RESUMES FOR THE 50+ JOB HUNTER

THIRD EDITION

RESUMES FOR

THE 50+ JOB HUNTER

The Editors of McGraw-Hill

Mc Graw Hill

New York Chicago San Francisco Lisbon London Madrid Mexico City
Milan New Delhi San Juan Seoul Singapore Sydney Toronto

Library of Congress Cataloging-in-Publication Data

Resumes for the 50+ job hunter / editors of McGraw-Hill. — 3rd ed.
    p.   cm.
ISBN-13: 978-0-07-154536-5 (alk. paper)
ISBN-10: 0-07-154536-0 (alk. paper)
1. Résumés (Employment)   2. Older people—Employment—United States.
3. Middle-aged persons—Employment—United States.   4. Age and
employment—United States.   I. McGraw-Hill Publishing Company.   II. Title:
Resumes for the fifty-plus job hunter.

HF5383.R453   2008
650.14'208460973—dc22   2008024668

2 3 4 5 6 7 8 9 10 11 12 13 14 15 16 17 18 19 20 21 QPD/QPD 0 9

ISBN 978-0-07-154536-5
MHID   0-07-154536-0

McGraw-Hill books are available at special quantity discounts to use as premiums and
sales promotions or for use in corporate training programs. To contact a representative,
please visit the Contact Us pages at www.mhprofessional.com.

This book is printed on acid-free paper.

Contents

Introduction

Your resume is a piece of paper (or an electronic document) that serves to introduce you to the people who will eventually hire you. To write a thoughtful resume, you must thoroughly assess your personality, your accomplishments, and the skills you have acquired. The act of composing and submitting a resume also requires you to carefully consider the company or individual that might hire you. What are they looking for, and how can you meet their needs? This book shows you how to organize your personal information and experience into a concise and well-written resume, so that your qualifications and potential as an employee will be understood easily and quickly by a complete stranger.

Writing the resume is just one step in what can be a daunting job search process, but it is an important element in the chain of events that will lead you to your new position. While you are probably a talented, bright, and charming person, your resume may not reflect these qualities. A poorly written resume can get you nowhere; a well-written resume can land you an interview and potentially a job. A good resume can even lead the interviewer to ask you questions that will allow you to talk about your strengths and highlight the skills you can bring to a prospective employer. Even a person with very little experience can find a good job if he or she is assisted by a thoughtful and polished resume.

Lengthy, typewritten resumes are a thing of the past. Today, employers do not have the time or the patience for verbose documents; they look for tightly composed, straightforward, action-based resumes. Although a one-page resume is the norm, a two-page resume may be warranted if you have had extensive job experience or have changed careers and truly need the space to properly position yourself. If, after careful editing, you still need more than one page to present yourself, it's acceptable to use a second page. A crowded resume that's hard to read would be the worst of your choices.

Distilling your work experience, education, and interests into such a small space requires preparation and planning. This book takes you step-by-step through the process of crafting an effective resume that will stand out in today's competitive marketplace. It serves as a workbook and a place to write down your experiences, while also including the techniques you'll need to pull all the necessary elements together. In the following pages, you'll find many examples of resumes that are specific to your area of interest. Study them for inspiration and find what appeals to you. There are a variety of ways to organize and present your information; inside, you'll find several that will be suitable to your needs. Good luck landing the job of your dreams.

The Elements of an Effective Resume

An effective resume is composed of information that employers are most interested in knowing about a prospective job applicant. This information is conveyed by a few essential elements. The following is a list of elements that are found in most resumes—some essential, some optional. Later in this chapter, we will further examine the role of each of these elements in the makeup of your resume.

- Heading

- Objective and/or Keyword Section

- Work Experience

- Education

- Honors

- Activities

- Certificates and Licenses

- Publications

- Professional Memberships

- Special Skills

- Personal Information

- References

The first step in preparing your resume is to gather information about yourself and your past accomplishments. Later you will refine this information, rewrite it using effective language, and organize it into an attractive layout. But first, let's take a look at each of these important elements individually so you can judge their appropriateness for your resume.

Heading

Although the heading may seem to be the simplest section of your resume, be careful not to take it lightly. It is the first section your prospective employer will see, and it contains the information she or he will need to contact you. At the very least, the heading must contain your name, your home address, and, of course, a phone number where you can be reached easily.

In today's high-tech world, many of us have multiple ways that we can be contacted. You may list your e-mail address if you are reasonably sure the employer makes use of this form of communication. Keep in mind, however, that others may have access to your e-mail messages if you send them from an account provided by your current company. If this is a concern, do not list your work e-mail address on your resume. If you are able to take calls at your current place of business, you should include your work number, because most employers will attempt to contact you during typical business hours.

If you have voice mail or a reliable answering machine at home or at work, list its number in the heading and make sure your greeting is professional and clear. Always include at least one phone number in your heading, even if it is a temporary number, where a prospective employer can leave a message.

You might have a dozen different ways to be contacted, but you do not need to list all of them. Confine your numbers or addresses to those that are the easiest for the prospective employer to use and the simplest for you to retrieve.

Objective

When seeking a specific career path, it is important to list a job or career objective on your resume. This statement helps employers know the direction you see yourself taking, so they can determine whether your goals are in line with those of their organization and the position available. Normally, an objective is one to two sentences long. Its contents will vary depending on your career field, goals, and personality. The objective can be specific or general, but it should always be to the point. See the sample resumes in this book for examples.

If you are planning to use this resume online, or you suspect your potential employer is likely to scan your resume, you will want to include a "keyword" in the objective. This allows a prospective employer, searching hundreds of resumes for a specific skill or position objective, to locate the keyword and find your resume. In essence, a keyword is what's "hot" in your particular field at a given time. It's a buzzword, a shorthand way of getting a particular message across at a glance. For example, if you are a lawyer, your objective might state your desire to work in the area of corporate litigation. In this case, someone searching for the keyword "corporate litigation" will pull up your resume and know that you want to plan, research, and present cases at trial on behalf of the corporation. If your objective states that you "desire a challenging position in systems design," the keyword is "systems design," an industry-specific shorthand way of saying that you want to be involved in assessing the need for, acquiring, and implementing high-technology systems. These are keywords and every industry has them, so it's becoming more and more important to include a few in your resume. (You may need to conduct additional research to make sure you know what keywords are most likely to be used in your desired industry, profession, or situation.)

There are many resume and job-search sites online. Like most things in the online world, they vary a great deal in quality. Use your discretion. If you plan to apply for jobs online or advertise your availability this way, you will want to design a scannable resume. This type of resume uses a format that can be easily scanned into a computer and added to a database. Scanning allows a prospective employer to use keywords to quickly review each applicant's experience and skills, and (in the event that there are many candidates for the job) to keep your resume for future reference.

Many people find that it is worthwhile to create two or more versions of their basic resume. You may want an intricately designed resume on high-quality paper to mail or hand out *and* a resume that is designed to be scanned into a computer and saved on a database or an online job site. You can even create a resume in ASCII text to e-mail to prospective employers. For further information, you may wish to refer to the *Guide to Internet Job Searching*, by Frances Roehm and Margaret Dikel, updated and published every other year by McGraw-Hill. This excellent book contains helpful and detailed information about formatting a resume for Internet use. To get you started, in Chapter 3 we have included a list of things to keep in mind when creating electronic resumes.

Although it is usually a good idea to include an objective, in some cases this element is not necessary. The goal of the objective statement is to provide the employer with an idea of where you see yourself going in the field. However, if you are uncertain of the exact nature of the job you seek, including an objective that is too specific could result in your not being considered for a host of perfectly acceptable positions. If you decide not to use an objective heading in your resume, you should definitely incorporate the information that would be conveyed in the objective into your cover letter.

Work Experience

Work experience is arguably the most important element of them all. Unless you are a recent graduate or former homemaker with little or no relevant work experience, your current and former positions will provide the central focus of the resume. You will want this section to be as complete and carefully constructed as possible. By thoroughly examining your work experience, you can get to the heart of your accomplishments and present them in a way that demonstrates and highlights your qualifications.

If you are just entering the workforce, your resume will probably focus on your education, but you should also include information on your work or volunteer experiences. Although you will have less information about work experience than a person who has held multiple positions or is advanced in his or her career, the amount of information is not what is most important in this section. How the information is presented and what it says about you as a worker and a person are what really count.

As you create this section of your resume, remember the need for accuracy. Include all the necessary information about each of your jobs, including your job title, dates of employment, name of your employer, city, state, responsibilities, special projects you handled, and accomplishments. Be sure to list only accomplishments for which you were directly responsible. And don't be alarmed if you haven't participated in or worked on special projects, because this section may not be relevant to certain jobs.

The most common way to list your work experience is in *reverse chronological order*. In other words, start with your most recent job and work your way backward. This way, your prospective employer sees your current (and often most important) position before considering your past employment. Your most recent position, if it's the most important in terms of responsibilities and relevance to the job for which you are applying, should also be the one that includes the most information as compared to your previous positions.

Even if the work itself seems unrelated to your proposed career path, you should list any job or experience that will help sell your talents. If you were promoted or given greater responsibilities or commendations, be sure to mention the fact.

The following worksheet is provided to help you organize your experiences in the working world. It will also serve as an excellent resource to refer to when updating your resume in the future.

WORK EXPERIENCE

Job One:

Job Title _____

Dates _____

Employer _____

City, State _____

Major Duties _____

_____

_____

_____

_____

_____

_____

_____

Special Projects _____

_____

_____

_____

Accomplishments _____

_____

_____

_____

_____

_____

Job Two:

Job Title _____

Dates _____

Employer _____

City, State _____

Major Duties _____

_____

_____

_____

_____

_____

_____

_____

Special Projects _____

_____

_____

_____

Accomplishments _____

_____

_____

_____

_____

_____

_____

_____

Job Three:

Job Title _____

Dates _____

Employer _____

City, State _____

Major Duties _____

_____

_____

_____

_____

_____

_____

_____

Special Projects _____

_____

_____

_____

Accomplishments _____

_____

_____

_____

_____

_____

_____

_____

Job Four:

Job Title _____

Dates _____

Employer _____

City, State _____

Major Duties _____

_____

_____

_____

_____

_____

_____

_____

Special Projects _____

_____

_____

_____

Accomplishments _____

_____

_____

_____

_____

_____

_____

_____

Education

Education is usually the second most important element of a resume. Your educational background is often a deciding factor in an employer's decision to interview you. Highlight your accomplishments in school as much as you did those accomplishments at work. If you are looking for your first professional job, your education or life experience will be your greatest asset because your related work experience will be minimal. In this case, the education section becomes the most important means of selling yourself.

Include in this section all the degrees or certificates you have received; your major or area of concentration; all of the honors you earned; and any relevant activities you participated in, organized, or chaired. Again, list your most recent schooling first. If you have completed graduate-level work, begin with that and work your way back through your undergraduate education. If you have completed college, you generally should not list your high-school experience; do so only if you earned special honors, you had a grade point average that was much better than the norm, or this was your highest level of education.

If you have completed a large number of credit hours in a subject that may be relevant to the position you are seeking but did not obtain a degree, you may wish to list the hours or classes you completed. Keep in mind, however, that you may be asked to explain why you did not finish the program. If you are currently in school, list the degree, certificate, or license you expect to obtain and the projected date of completion.

The following worksheet will help you gather the information you need for this section of your resume.

EDUCATION

School One _____

Major or Area of Concentration _____

Degree _____

Dates _____

School Two _____

Major or Area of Concentration _____

Degree _____

Dates _____

Honors

If you include an honors section in your resume, you should highlight any awards, honors, or memberships in honorary societies that you have received. (You may also incorporate this information into your education section.) Often, the honors are academic in nature, but this section also may be used for special achievements in sports, clubs, or other school activities. Always include the name of the organization awarding the honor and the date(s) received. Use the following worksheet to help you gather your information.

HONORS

Honor One _____

Awarding Organization _____

Date(s) _____

Honor Two _____

Awarding Organization _____

Date(s) _____

Honor Three _____

Awarding Organization _____

Date(s) _____

Honor Four _____

Awarding Organization _____

Date(s) _____

Honor Five _____

Awarding Organization _____

Date(s) _____

Activities

Perhaps you have been active in different organizations or clubs; often an employer will look at such involvement as evidence of initiative, dedication, and good social skills. Examples of your ability to take a leading role in a group should be included on a resume, if you can provide them. The activities section of your resume should present neighborhood and community activities, volunteer positions, and so forth. In general, you may want to avoid listing any organization whose name indicates the race, creed, sex, age, marital status, sexual orientation, or nation of origin of its members because this could expose you to discrimination. Use the following worksheet to list the specifics of your activities.

ACTIVITIES

Organization/Activity _____

Accomplishments _____

_____

_____

Organization/Activity _____

Accomplishments _____

_____

_____

Organization/Activity _____

Accomplishments _____

_____

_____

As your work experience grows through the years, your school activities and honors will carry less weight and be emphasized less in your resume. Eventually, you will probably list only your degree and any major honors received. As time goes by, your job performance and the experience you've gained become the most important elements in your resume, which should change to reflect this.

Certificates and Licenses

If your chosen career path requires specialized training, you may already have certificates or licenses. You should list these if the job you are seeking requires them and you, of course, have acquired them. If you have applied for a license but have not yet received it, use the phrase "application pending."

License requirements vary by state. If you have moved or are planning to relocate to another state, check with that state's board or licensing agency for all licensing requirements.

Always make sure that all of the information you list is completely accurate. Locate copies of your certificates and licenses, and check the exact date and name of the accrediting agency. Use the following worksheet to organize the necessary information.

CERTIFICATES AND LICENSES

Name of License _____

Licensing Agency _____

Date Issued _____

Name of License _____

Licensing Agency _____

Date Issued _____

Name of License _____

Licensing Agency _____

Date Issued _____

Publications

Some professions strongly encourage or even require that you publish. If you have written, coauthored, or edited any books, articles, professional papers, or works of a similar nature that pertain to your field, you will definitely want to include this element. Remember to list the date of publication and the publisher's name, and specify whether you were the sole author or a coauthor. Book, magazine, or journal titles are generally italicized, while the titles of articles within a larger publication appear in quotes. (Check with your reference librarian for more about the appropriate way to present this information.) For scientific or research papers, you will need to give the date, place, and audience to whom the paper was presented.

Use the following worksheet to help you gather the necessary information about your publications.

PUBLICATIONS

Title and Type (Note, Article, etc.) _____

Title of Publication (Journal, Book, etc.) _____

Publisher _____

Date Published _____

Title and Type (Note, Article, etc.) _____

Title of Publication (Journal, Book, etc.) _____

Publisher _____

Date Published _____

Title and Type (Note, Article, etc.) _____

Title of Publication (Journal, Book, etc.) _____

Publisher _____

Date Published _____

Professional Memberships

Another potential element in your resume is a section listing professional memberships. Use this section to describe your involvement in professional associations, unions, and similar organizations. It is to your advantage to list any professional memberships that pertain to the job you are seeking. Many employers see your membership as representative of your desire to stay up-to-date and connected in your field. Include the dates of your involvement and whether you took part in any special activities or held any offices within the organization. Use the following worksheet to organize your information.

PROFESSIONAL MEMBERSHIPS

Name of Organization _____

Office(s) Held_____

Activities _____

Dates _____

Name of Organization _____

Office(s) Held_____

Activities _____

Dates _____

Name of Organization _____

Office(s) Held_____

Activities _____

Dates _____

Name of Organization _____

Office(s) Held_____

Activities _____

Dates _____

Special Skills

The special skills section of your resume is the place to mention any special abilities you have that relate to the job you are seeking. You can use this element to present certain talents or experiences that are not necessarily a part of your education or work experience. Common examples include fluency in a foreign language, extensive travel abroad, or knowledge of a particular computer application. "Special skills" can encompass a wide range of talents, and this section can be used creatively. However, for each skill you list, you should be able to describe how it would be a direct asset in the type of work you're seeking because employers may ask just that in an interview. If you can't think of a way to do this, it may be extraneous information.

Personal Information

Some people include personal information on their resumes. This is generally not recommended, but you might wish to include it if you think that something in your personal life, such as a hobby or talent, has some bearing on the position you are seeking. This type of information is often referred to at the beginning of an interview, when it may be used as an icebreaker. Of course, personal information regarding your age, marital status, race, religion, or sexual orientation should never appear on your resume as personal information. It should be given only in the context of memberships and activities, and only when doing so would not expose you to discrimination.

References

References are not usually given on the resume itself, but a prospective employer needs to know that you have references who may be contacted if necessary. All you need to include is a single sentence at the end of the resume: "References are available upon request," or even simply, "References available." Have a reference list ready—your interviewer may ask to see it! Contact each person on the list ahead of time to see whether it is all right for you to use him or her as a reference. This way, the person has a chance to think about what to say *before* the call occurs. This helps ensure that you will obtain the best reference possible.

Chapter 2

Writing Your Resume

N ow that you have gathered the information for each section of your resume, it's time to write it out in a way that will get the attention of the reviewer—hopefully, your future employer! The language you use in your resume will affect its success, so you must be careful and conscientious. Translate the facts you have gathered into the active, precise language of resume writing. You will be aiming for a resume that keeps the reader's interest and highlights your accomplishments in a concise and effective way.

Resume writing is unlike any other form of writing. Although your seventh-grade composition teacher would not approve, the rules of punctuation and sentence building are often completely ignored. Instead, you should try for a functional, direct writing style that focuses on the use of verbs and other words that imply action on your part. Writing with action words and strong verbs characterizes you to potential employers as an energetic, active person, someone who completes tasks and achieves results from his or her work. Resumes that do not make use of action words can sound passive and stale. These resumes are not effective and do not get the attention of any employer, no matter how qualified the applicant. Choose words that display your strengths and demonstrate your initiative. The following list of commonly used verbs will help you create a strong resume:

administered	assembled
advised	assumed responsibility
analyzed	billed
arranged	built

carried out	inspected
channeled	interviewed
collected	introduced
communicated	invented
compiled	maintained
completed	managed
conducted	met with
contacted	motivated
contracted	negotiated
coordinated	operated
counseled	orchestrated
created	ordered
cut	organized
designed	oversaw
determined	performed
developed	planned
directed	prepared
dispatched	presented
distributed	produced
documented	programmed
edited	published
established	purchased
expanded	recommended
functioned as	recorded
gathered	reduced
handled	referred
hired	represented
implemented	researched
improved	reviewed

saved	supervised
screened	taught
served as	tested
served on	trained
sold	typed
suggested	wrote

Let's look at two examples that differ only in their writing style. The first resume section is ineffective because it does not use action words to accent the applicant's work experiences.

WORK EXPERIENCE
Regional Sales Manager

Manager of sales representatives from seven states. Manager of twelve food chain accounts in the East. In charge of the sales force's planned selling toward specific goals. Supervisor and trainer of new sales representatives. Consulting for customers in the areas of inventory management and quality control.

Special Projects: Coordinator and sponsor of annual Food Industry Seminar.

Accomplishments: Monthly regional volume went up 25 percent during my tenure while, at the same time, a proper sales/cost ratio was maintained. Customer-company relations were improved.

In the following paragraph, we have rewritten the same section using action words. Notice how the tone has changed. It now sounds stronger and more active. This person accomplished goals and really *did* things.

WORK EXPERIENCE
Regional Sales Manager

Managed sales representatives from seven states. Oversaw twelve food chain accounts in the eastern United States. Directed the sales force in planned selling toward specific goals. Supervised and trained new sales representatives. Counseled customers in the areas of inventory management and quality control. Coordinated and sponsored the annual Food Industry Seminar. Increased monthly regional volume by 25 percent and helped to improve customer-company relations during my tenure.

One helpful way to construct the work experience section is to make use of your actual job descriptions—the written duties and expectations your employers have for a person in your current or former position. Job descriptions are rarely written in proper resume language, so you will have to rework them, but they do include much of the information necessary to create this section of your resume. If you have access to job descriptions for your former positions, you can use the details to construct an action-oriented paragraph. Often, your human resources department can provide a job description for your current position.

The following is an example of a typical human resources job description, followed by a rewritten version of the same description employing action words and specific details about the job. Again, pay attention to the style of writing instead of the content, as the details of your own experience will be unique.

WORK EXPERIENCE
Public Administrator I

Responsibilities: Coordinate and direct public services to meet the needs of the nation, state, or community. Analyze problems; work with special committees and public agencies; recommend solutions to governing bodies.

Aptitudes and Skills: Ability to relate to and communicate with people; solve complex problems through analysis; plan, organize, and implement policies and programs. Knowledge of political systems, financial management, personnel administration, program evaluation, and organizational theory.

WORK EXPERIENCE
Public Administrator I

Wrote pamphlets and conducted discussion groups to inform citizens of legislative processes and consumer issues. Organized and supervised 25 interviewers. Trained interviewers in effective communication skills.

After you have written out your resume, you are ready to begin the next important step: assembly and layout.

Assembly and Layout

A t this point, you've gathered all the necessary information for your resume and rewritten it in language that will impress your potential employers. Your next step is to assemble the sections in a logical order and lay them out on the page neatly and attractively to achieve the desired effect: getting the interview.

Assembly

The order of the elements in a resume makes a difference in its overall effect. Clearly, you would not want to bury your name and address somewhere in the middle of the resume. Nor would you want to lead with a less important section, such as special skills. Put the elements in an order that stresses your most important accomplishments and the things that will be most appealing to your potential employer. For example, if you are new to the workforce, you will want the reviewer to read about your education and life skills before any part-time jobs you may have held for short durations. On the other hand, if you have been gainfully employed for several years and currently hold an important position in your company, you should list your work accomplishments ahead of your educational information, which has become less pertinent with time.

Certain things should always be included in your resume, but others are optional. The following list shows you which are which. You might want to use it as a checklist to be certain that you have included all of the necessary information.

Essential	**Optional**
Name	Cellular Phone Number
Address	Pager Number
Phone Number	E-Mail Address or Website Address
Work Experience	Voice Mail Number
Education	Job Objective
References Phrase	Honors
	Special Skills
	Publications
	Professional Memberships
	Activities
	Certificates and Licenses
	Personal Information
	Graphics
	Photograph

Your choice of optional sections depends on your own background and employment needs. Always use information that will put you in a favorable light—unless it's absolutely essential, avoid anything that will prompt the interviewer to ask questions about your weaknesses or something else that could be unflattering. Make sure your information is accurate and truthful. If your honors are impressive, include them in the resume. If your activities in school demonstrate talents that are necessary for the job you are seeking, allow space for a section on activities. If you are applying for a position that requires ornamental illustration, you may want to include border illustrations or graphics that demonstrate your talents in this area. If you are answering an advertisement for a job that requires certain physical traits, a photo of yourself might be appropriate. A person applying for a job as a computer programmer would *not* include a photo as part of his or her resume. Each resume is unique, just as each person is unique.

Types of Resumes

So far we have focused on the most common type of resume—the *reverse chronological* resume—in which your most recent job is listed first. This is the type of resume usually preferred by those who have to read a large number of resumes, and it is by far the most popular and widely circulated. However, this style of presentation may not be the most effective way to highlight *your* skills and accomplishments.

For example, if you are reentering the workforce after many years or are trying to change career fields, the *functional* resume may work best. This type of resume puts the focus on your achievements instead of the sequence of your work history. In the functional resume, your experience is presented through your general accomplishments and the skills you have developed in your working life.

A functional resume is assembled from the same information you gathered in Chapter 1. The main difference lies in how you organize the information. Essentially, the work experience section is divided in two, with your job duties and accomplishments constituting one section and your employers' names, cities, and states; your positions; and the dates employed making up the other. Place the first section near the top of your resume, just below your job objective (if used), and call it *Accomplishments* or *Achievements*. The second section, containing the bare essentials of your work history, should come after the accomplishments section and can be called *Employment History*, since it is a chronological overview of your former jobs.

The other sections of your resume remain the same. The work experience section is the only one affected in the functional format. By placing the section that focuses on your achievements at the beginning, you draw attention to these achievements. This puts less emphasis on where you worked and when, and more on what you did and what you are capable of doing.

If you are changing careers, the emphasis on skills and achievements is important. The identities of previous employers (who aren't part of your new career field) need to be downplayed. A functional resume can help accomplish this task. If you are reentering the workforce after a long absence, a functional resume is the obvious choice. And if you lack full-time work experience, you will need to draw attention away from this fact and put the focus on your skills and abilities. You may need to highlight your volunteer activities and part-time work. Education may also play a more important role in your resume.

The type of resume that is right for you will depend on your personal circumstances. It may be helpful to create both types and then compare them. Which one presents you in the best light? Examples of both types of resumes are included in this book. Use the sample resumes in Chapter 5 to help you decide on the content, presentation, and look of your own resume.

Resume or Curriculum Vitae?

A curriculum vitae (CV) is a longer, more detailed synopsis of your professional history that generally runs three or more pages in length. It includes a summary of your educational and academic background as well as teaching and research experience, publications, presentations, awards, honors, affiliations, and other details. Because the purpose of the CV is different from that of the resume, many of the rules we've discussed thus far involving style and length do not apply.

A curriculum vitae is used primarily for admissions applications to graduate or professional schools, independent consulting in a variety of settings, proposals for fellowships or grants, or applications for positions in academia. As with a resume, you may need different versions of a CV for different types of positions. You should only send a CV when one is specifically requested by an employer or institution.

Like a resume, your CV should include your name, contact information, education, skills, and experience. In addition to the basics, a CV includes research and teaching experience, publications, grants and fellowships, professional associations and licenses, awards, and other information relevant to the position for which you are applying. You can follow the advice presented thus far to gather and organize your personal information.

Special Tips for Electronic Resumes

Because there are many details to consider in writing a resume that will be posted or transmitted on the Internet, or one that will be scanned into a computer when it is received, we suggest that you refer to the *Guide to Internet Job Searching*, by Frances Roehm and Margaret Dikel, as previously mentioned. However, here are some brief, general guidelines to follow if you expect your resume to be scanned into a computer.

- Use standard fonts in which none of the letters touch.

- Keep in mind that underlining, italics, and fancy scripts may not scan well.

- Use boldface and capitalization to set off elements. Again, make sure letters don't touch. Leave at least a quarter inch between lines of type.

- Keep information and elements at the left margin. Centering, columns, and even indenting may change when the resume is optically scanned.

- Do not use any lines, boxes, or graphics.

- Place the most important information at the top of the first page. If you use two pages, put "Page 1 of 2" at the bottom of the first page and put your name and "Page 2 of 2" at the top of the second page.

- List each telephone number on its own line in the header.

- Use multiple keywords or synonyms for what you do to make sure your qualifications will be picked up if a prospective employer is searching for them. Use nouns that are keywords for your profession.

- Be descriptive in your titles. For example, don't just use "assistant"; use "legal office assistant."

- Make sure the contrast between print and paper is good. Use a high-quality laser printer and white or very light colored 8½-by-11-inch paper.

- Mail a high-quality laser print or an excellent copy. Do not fold or use staples, as this might interfere with scanning. You may, however, use paper clips.

In addition to creating a resume that works well for scanning, you may want to have a resume that can be e-mailed to reviewers. Because you may not know what word processing application the recipient uses, the best format to use is ASCII text. (ASCII stands for "American Standard Code for Information Interchange.") It allows people with very different software platforms to exchange and understand information. (E-mail operates on this principle.) ASCII is a simple, text-only language, which means you can include only simple text. There can be no use of boldface, italics, or even paragraph indentations.

To create an ASCII resume, just use your normal word processing program; when finished, save it as a "text only" document. You will find this option under the "save" or "save as" command. Here is a list of things to *avoid* when crafting your electronic resume:

- Tabs. Use your space bar. Tabs will not work.

- Any special characters, such as mathematical symbols.

- Word wrap. Use hard returns (the return key) to make line breaks.

- Centering or other formatting. Align everything at the left margin.

- Bold or italic fonts. Everything will be converted to plain text when you save the file as a "text only" document.

Check carefully for any mistakes before you save the document as a text file. Spellcheck and proofread it several times; then ask someone with a keen eye to go over it again for you. Remember: the key is to keep it simple. Any attempt to make this resume pretty or decorative may result in a resume that is confusing and hard to read. After you have saved the document, you can cut and paste it into an e-mail or onto a website.

Layout for a Paper Resume

A great deal of care—and much more formatting—is necessary to achieve an attractive layout for your paper resume. There is no single appropriate layout that applies to every resume, but there are a few basic rules to follow in putting your resume on paper:

- Leave a comfortable margin on the sides, top, and bottom of the page (usually one to one and a half inches).

- Use appropriate spacing between the sections (two to three line spaces are usually adequate).

- Be consistent in the *type* of headings you use for different sections of your resume. For example, if you capitalize the heading EMPLOYMENT HISTORY, don't use initial capitals and underlining for a section of equal importance, such as Education.

- Do not use more than one font in your resume. Stay consistent by choosing a font that is fairly standard and easy to read, and don't change it for different sections. Beware of the tendency to try to make your resume original by choosing fancy type styles; your resume may end up looking unprofessional instead of creative. Unless you are in a very creative and artistic field, you should almost always stick with tried-and-true type styles like Times New Roman and Palatino, which are often used in business writing. In the area of resume styles, conservative is usually the best way to go.

CHRONOLOGICAL RESUME

SARAH JENNINGS

12 Barkley Place • Chicago, Illinois 60652 • (773) 555-2114 • sarahjennings@xxx.com

OBJECTIVE

A position in retailing

EXPERIENCE

Lendman's Department Stores, 1999 to present

1986 to present • Assistant Manager, Home Furnishings

• Responsible for sales, merchandising, and customer service.

• Assist customers in selecting home furnishings to meet their personal needs.

• Supervise a staff of seven sales assistants and merchandise clerks.

• Provide customer feedback to the corporate buying department and assist in the selection of new items.

1999 to 2006 • Sales Clerk, Home Furnishings

• Twice selected "Employee of the Month."

• Increased sales by 7 percent while reducing customer complaints by 30 percent.

• Selected to participate on a task force designed to improve selection and customer service in the home furnishings area.

1981 to 1999 • Homemaker

• Raised three children and held leadership positions in a variety of civic organizations.

• Active in the Chicago area YWCA, United Way Campaign, and other charitable causes.

• Served as United Way Membership Chairperson in 1995.

• Received a mayoral citation for excellent service.

1978 to 1981 • Sales Clerk, Women's Clothing, Yauckey's Department Stores

• Assisted customers in selection and clothing sales.

• Supervised junior sales clerks.

• Handled timecards and check disbursement for owner.

References available upon request.

FUNCTIONAL RESUME

ROBERT CHEKOV
522 Market Street, Lewisburg, PA 17837   Home: (709) 555-8877
Email: robertchekov@xxx.com   Cell: (709) 555-7115

SUMMARY
- More than thirty years of progressive management and marketing experience within demanding business environments.
- Proven ability to assess organizational need and implement effective administrative procedures.
- Multilingual; experienced communicating with varied cultures and all levels within an organization.
- Proficient at working independently, handling simultaneous projects, and meeting deadlines.
- Strong management, problem-solving, and supervisory skills.

ACCOMPLISHMENTS
- Provided technical and advisory support to manufacturing plants.
- Participated in alternate supplier approvals.
- Increased departmental output by 50 percent.
- Developed and implemented a new format for ingredient specifications.
- Doubled projected sales volume for an international office supply firm.
- Directed all business activities for a highly profitable textile manufacturing organization.
- Devised innovative and highly efficient methods of optimizing raw materials.
- Increased net profits from 12 percent to 35 percent, and increased productivity of manufactured products by 40 percent.

EMPLOYMENT

Specifications Technologist	American Home Products	1985 to present
Division Manager	SP Clobus/SP Coopprom	1979 to 1984
Sales Broker	Sales Distribution Co.	1978 to 1979
Medical Support	Bulgarian Armed Forces	1976 to 1978

EDUCATION

M.S. International Business, Bucknell University, Lewisburg, PA	1980
B.S., Higher Medical Institute of Pleven, Medical Academy, Bulgaria	1968

LANGUAGES
Fluent in English, German, Bulgarian
Conversant in Russian and Macedonian

REFERENCES AVAILABLE ON REQUEST

- Always try to fit your resume on one page. If you are having trouble with this, you may be trying to say too much. Edit out any repetitive or unnecessary information, and shorten descriptions of earlier jobs where possible. Ask a friend you trust for feedback on what seems unnecessary or unimportant. For example, you may have included too many optional sections. Today, with the prevalence of the personal computer as a tool, there is no excuse for a poorly laid out resume. Experiment with variations until you are pleased with the result.

Remember that a resume is not an autobiography. Too much information will only get in the way. The more compact your resume, the easier it will be to review. If a person who is swamped with resumes looks at yours, catches the main points, and then calls you for an interview to fill in some of the details, your resume has already accomplished its task. A clear and concise resume makes for a happy reader and a good impression.

There are times when, despite extensive editing, the resume simply cannot fit on one page. In this case, the resume should be laid out on two pages in such a way that neither clarity nor appearance is compromised. Each page of a two-page resume should be marked clearly: the first should indicate "Page 1 of 2," and the second should include your name and the page number, for example, "Julia Ramirez—Page 2 of 2." The pages should then be paper-clipped together. You may use a smaller type size (in the same font as the body of your resume) for the page numbers. Place them at the bottom of page one and the top of page two. Again, spend the time now to experiment with the layout until you find one that looks good to you.

Always show your final layout to other people and ask them what they like or dislike about it, and what impresses them most when they read your resume. Make sure that their responses are the same as what you want to elicit from your prospective employer. If they aren't the same, you should continue to make changes until the necessary information is emphasized.

Proofreading

After you have finished typing the master copy of your resume and before you have it copied or printed, thoroughly check it for typing and spelling errors. Do not place all your trust in your computer's spellcheck function. Use an old editing trick and read the whole resume backward—start at the end and read it right to left and bottom to top. This can help you see the small errors or inconsistencies that are easy to overlook. Take time to do it right because a single error on a document this important can cause the reader to judge your attention to detail in a harsh light.

Have several people look at the finished resume just in case you've missed an error. Don't try to take a shortcut; not having an unbiased set of eyes examine your resume now could mean embarrassment later. Even experienced editors can easily overlook their own errors. Be thorough and conscientious with your proofreading so your first impression is a perfect one.

We have included the following rules of capitalization and punctuation to assist you in the final stage of creating your resume. Remember that resumes often require use of a shorthand style of writing that may include sentences without periods and other stylistic choices that break the standard rules of grammar. Be consistent in each section and throughout the whole resume with your choices.

RULES OF CAPITALIZATION

- Capitalize proper nouns, such as names of schools, colleges, and universities; names of companies; and brand names of products.

- Capitalize major words in the names and titles of books, tests, and articles that appear in the body of your resume.

- Capitalize words in major section headings of your resume.

- Do not capitalize words just because they seem important.

- When in doubt, consult a style manual such as *Words into Type* (Prentice Hall) or *The Chicago Manual of Style* (The University of Chicago Press). Your local library can help you locate these and other reference books. Many computer programs also have grammar help sections.

RULES OF PUNCTUATION

- Use commas to separate words in a series.

- Use a semicolon to separate series of words that already include commas within the series. (For an example, see the first rule of capitalization.)

- Use a semicolon to separate independent clauses that are not joined by a conjunction.

- Use a period to end a sentence.

- Use a colon to show that examples or details follow that will expand or amplify the preceding phrase.

- Avoid the use of dashes.

- Avoid the use of brackets.

- If you use any punctuation in an unusual way in your resume, be consistent in its use.

- Whenever you are uncertain, consult a style manual.

Putting Your Resume in Print

You will need to buy high-quality paper for your printer before you print your finished resume. Regular office paper is not good enough for resumes; the reviewer will probably think it looks flimsy and cheap. Go to an office supply store or copy shop and select a high-quality bond paper that will make a good first impression. Select colors like white, off-white, or possibly a light gray. In some industries, a pastel may be acceptable, but be sure the color and feel of the paper make a subtle, positive statement about you. Nothing in the choice of paper should be loud or unprofessional.

If your computer printer does not reproduce your resume properly and produces smudged or stuttered type, either ask to borrow a friend's or take your disk (or a clean original) to a printer or copy shop for high-quality copying. If you anticipate needing a large number of copies, taking your resume to a copy shop or a printer is probably the best choice.

Hold a sheet of your unprinted bond paper up to the light. If it has a watermark, you will want to point this out to the person helping you with copies; the printing should be done so that the reader can read the print and see the watermark the right way up. Check each copy for smudges or streaks. This is the time to be a perfectionist—the results of your careful preparation will be well worth it.

Chapter

4

The Cover Letter

Once your resume has been assembled, laid out, and printed to your satisfaction, the next and final step before distribution is to write your cover letter. Though there may be instances where you deliver your resume in person, you will usually send it through the mail or online. Resumes sent through the mail always need an accompanying letter that briefly introduces you and your resume. The purpose of the cover letter is to get a potential employer to read your resume, just as the purpose of the resume is to get that same potential employer to call you for an interview.

Like your resume, your cover letter should be clean, neat, and direct. A cover letter usually includes the following information:

1. Your name and address (unless it already appears on your personal letterhead) and your phone number(s); see item 7.

2. The date.

3. The name and address of the person and company to whom you are sending your resume.

4. The salutation ("Dear Mr." or "Dear Ms." followed by the person's last name, or "To Whom It May Concern" if you are answering a blind ad).

5. An opening paragraph explaining why you are writing (for example, in response to an ad, as a follow-up to a previous meeting, at the suggestion of someone you both know) and indicating that you are interested in whatever job is being offered.

6. One or more paragraphs that tell why you want to work for the company and what qualifications and experiences you can bring to the position. This is a good place to mention some detail about

that particular company that makes you want to work for them; this shows that you have done some research before applying.

7. A final paragraph that closes the letter and invites the reviewer to contact you for an interview. This can be a good place to tell the potential employer which method would be best to use when contacting you. Be sure to give the correct phone number and a good time to reach you, if that is important. You may mention here that your references are available upon request.

8. The closing ("Sincerely" or "Yours truly") followed by your signature in a dark ink, with your name typed under it.

Your cover letter should include all of this information and be no longer than one page in length. The language used should be polite, businesslike, and to the point. Don't attempt to tell your life story in the cover letter; a long and cluttered letter will serve only to annoy the reader. Remember that you need to mention only a few of your accomplishments and skills in the cover letter. The rest of your information is available in your resume. If your cover letter is a success, your resume will be read and all pertinent information reviewed by your prospective employer.

Producing the Cover Letter

Cover letters should always be individualized because they are always written to specific individuals and companies. Never use a form letter for your cover letter or copy it as you would a resume. Each cover letter should be unique, and as personal and lively as possible. (Of course, once you have written and rewritten your first cover letter until you are satisfied with it, you can certainly use similar wording in subsequent letters. You may want to save a template on your computer for future reference.) Keep a hard copy of each cover letter so you know exactly what you wrote in each one.

There are sample cover letters in Chapter 6. Use them as models or for ideas of how to assemble and lay out your own cover letters. Remember that every letter is unique and depends on the particular circumstances of the individual writing it and the job for which he or she is applying.

After you have written your cover letter, proofread it as thoroughly as you did your resume. Again, spelling or punctuation errors are a sure sign of carelessness, and you don't want that to be a part of your first impression on a prospective employer. This is no time to trust your spellcheck function. Even after going through a spelling and grammar check, your cover letter should be carefully proofread by at least one other person.

Print the cover letter on the same quality bond paper you used for your resume. Remember to sign it, using a good dark-ink pen. Handle the letter and resume carefully to avoid smudging or wrinkling, and mail them together in an appropriately sized envelope. Many stores sell matching envelopes to coordinate with your choice of bond paper.

Keep an accurate record of all resumes you send out and the results of each mailing. This record can be kept on your computer, in a calendar or notebook, or on file cards. Knowing when a resume is likely to have been received will keep you on track as you make follow-up phone calls.

About a week after mailing resumes and cover letters to potential employers, contact them by telephone. Confirm that your resume arrived and ask whether an interview might be possible. Be sure to record the name of the person you spoke to and any other information you gleaned from the conversation. It is wise to treat the person answering the phone with a great deal of respect; sometimes the assistant or receptionist has the ear of the person doing the hiring.

You should make a great impression with the strong, straightforward resume and personalized cover letter you have just created. We wish you every success in securing the career of your dreams!

Chapter 5

Sample Resumes

This chapter contains dozens of sample resumes for people pursuing a wide variety of jobs and careers.

There are many different styles of resumes in terms of graphic layout and presentation of information. These samples represent people with varying amounts of education and experience. Use them as models for your own resume. Choose one resume or borrow elements from several different resumes to help you construct your own.

Earl Mobley Jr.

13 Paddock Drive • Ernest, LA 33323

(806) 555-3547 • Cell: (806) 555-1466 • earlmobley@xxx.com

Experience

Rochelle Food Products, 1988–present

General Manager, Specialty Products Division

- Overall P&L responsibility for the day-to-day operations of the specialty products division. This includes direction of the operations, manufacturing, and distribution departments, which produce a variety of derivatives used by food and beverage manufacturers. Inherited a large commodity business where the ability to control costs was crucial for survival.

- Increased production to lower unit costs, thus enabling the division to take advantage of growth in the market, increase market share, and substitute for higher-cost production in the U.S.

- Successfully addressed a wide range of internal problems including labor relations, high employee absenteeism, restrictive labor practices, and safety issues.

- Introduced the largest industrial product treatment plan in company history for processing waste products.

- Succeeded in increasing plant output by 46 percent and reducing product cost by 23 percent.

Earlier positions included:

- Director of Production
- Director of Engineering
- Process and Project Engineering Manager
- Process Engineering Manager
- Process Engineer

TRG-Imperial Products Division, 1984–1988

Section Leader

- Provided technical support to manufacturing operations.

- Created mathematical models, performed statistical analyses, built pilot plant to enhance product quality, and developed sophisticated controls and systems to reduce operation risk.

Education

M.B.A., Lockmount University

B.E. in Chemistry, Fairfield University

B.A. in History, Fairfield University

References available upon request.

SANDRA PATTERSON

12 OLD TOWN WAY	HOME: (607) 555-8977
PITTSBURGH, PA 56332	CELL: (607) 555-5892
EMAIL: SANDRAPATTERSON@XXX.COM	

Armore Foods, Subsidiary of Flastern Soup Company, 1981–Present

Vice President, Business Planning & Development, 2000–Present
- Created planning process to improve participation, input, and timeliness of strategic and operating plans.
- Developed direction for reducing short-term and long-term costs by more than $35 million annually. This plan contributed significantly to a 49 percent increase in earnings in fiscal year 2002.
- Evaluated and pursued acquisition candidates up to $100 million annual sales volume.

Vice President, Marketing, 1996–2000
- Developed professional management team and refocused department for integrated marketing programs.
- Achieved $6 million annual savings in nonproductive trade support by supervising development of scanner databased trade promotion evaluation systems.
- Key player in the evaluation of successful acquisitions with total sales volume of $175 million.

Group Brand Manager, New Products, 1988–1996
- Reduced potential cash flow losses by discontinuing several inherited projects.
- Launched product that used new manufacturing process to convert refrigerated products to dry shelf entry.

Marketing Manager, 1982–1988
- Developed a new product introduction that achieved $145 million in sales in its first year of introduction.
- Repositioned existing products resulting in a 23 percent increase in market penetration and sales.

Sales Representative, 1981–1982
- Successfully marketed company products in the Midwest and Eastern regions of the U.S.
- Developed an innovative sales training process still in use by the company.

EDUCATION

J. L. Kellogg Graduate School, Northwestern University: M.B.A., 1981
University of Chicago, B.A. Philosophy, B.S. Business: 1979

References available upon request.

WILLIAM ALLENBERG

2800 Plaza Drive
Torrance, CA 90556
(310) 555-7653
William.Allenberg@xxx.com

PROFESSIONAL CAPABILITIES

Skill with the following systems: Alliant FX, Alliant GX4000, Solaris, XServe, and VMware
Programming skills in the following operating systems and languages: Windows, Linux, C++, Perl, Oracle, and Java

PROFESSIONAL POSITIONS

Project Manager, 10/01–present
Simplified Optical Inc., Owab, CA 90744

- Responsible for designing, coding, installing, and maintaining software programs
- Assisted in the identification, evaluation, tailoring, and implementation of vendor-supplied software packages
- Evaluated the performance of installed software by utilizing available aids to monitor trends, loads, and growth patterns
- Analyzed dumps and applied fix procedures
- Prepared documentation for use by computer operations, applications programming, and user personnel

Systems Analyst, 1/97–10/01
Alliant Systems, Carson, CA 90503

- Provided technical assistance and information to other systems software, computer operations, applications programming, and data communications personnel at all centers with this environment
- Assisted the training of applications programming and user personnel in the use of software and related hardware facilities
- Reviewed new design enhancements and programs with systems analysts and applications programming personnel for operating efficiencies
- Assisted in design, coding, and installation of database management systems

Systems Analyst, 10/94–1/97
Mould CSD, Canoga Park, CA 91303

- Analyzed specifications for applications enhancements for compatibility with other systems and within operating guidelines
- Responsible for the hiring, firing, assessment, and rewarding of direct reports

Programmer, 10/89–10/94
Programmer, Syntec Corp., Van Nuys, CA 91411

- Created enterprise-level web applications
- Worked on a "can do" team in a rapid development environment

EDUCATIONAL BACKGROUND

M.B.A., April 1989
Pepperdine University, Malibu, CA

B.S., Computer Science, December 1984
State University of New York College of Technology, Utica, NY

References provided on request

TERRELL BROWN

118 21st Place • Jackson Beach, CA 90266 • 213-555-3815 • t.brown@xxx.com

Seasoned sales and marketing competitor with highly developed instincts for what will sell. Strong record of success with channel marketing and system-level sales in North America and international markets. Accomplished in managing sales teams and indirect sales forces. Effective in utilizing analytical skills to organize marketing plans, sales strategies, and resolution of marketing resource issues at the executive level.

1999 to present
Director of International Marketing, Lackland Technology Corporation
- Directed North American and international sales in Japan, Mexico, and South America for fault-tolerant client server in corporate MIS departments. Defined market and sales strategies that accounted for 50 percent of corporate revenues.
- Defined economic market size and available market for fault-tolerant client server in corporate MIS departments in North America. Directed the sale of $2 million in hardware components during the first 60-day promotional rollout.
- Developed and implemented sales plans and channel pricing strategies to boost North American sales.
- Managed and structured channel communication program and developed a direct sales program to banks and other financial institutions.

1988 to 1999
Marketing and Sales Manager, Trecor Manufacturing, Inc.
- Managed the overall sales for a $225 million division engaged in the development of telecommunications systems.
- Directed a national sales and marketing program for a new product line that resulted in identification of $30 million in new sales opportunities.
- Evaluated the feasibility of developing international alliances to improve market penetration into Pacific Rim countries.

1979 to 1988
Territory Sales Representative, Inman Heavy Equipment
- Marketed the company's construction-related products in a five-state region.
- Successfully opened 35 new accounts in the previously untested Oregon marketplace.

EDUCATION

B.A. Economics, Cornell University, 1979
Awarded Arthur Finkin National Scholarship

References available upon request.

WANDA KNIGHT
3884 Fairfax Court • Atlanta, Georgia 30339 • 404-555-7139 •
Wanda_Knight@xxx.com

EXPERIENCE
Arthritis Foundation National Office, Atlanta, Georgia, 1998 to present
Vice President, Corporate Relations
- Direct national foundation development activities through extensive interaction with executive management of leading business corporations.
- Oversee the development and implementation of corporate marketing and fundraising programs.
- Manage a staff of 35 through four direct reports.
- Manage a budget of $12 million.
- Increased corporate fundraising from $1.5 million to more than $4 million in a three-year period.

Ducky-Cola U.S.A., Atlanta, Georgia, 1990 to 1998
National Sales Manager, Chain Supermarkets/Convenience Stores
- Oversaw national sales and marketing of cola products to convenience stores and supermarket chains. Successfully expanded sales and share in each trade channel for five consecutive years.
- Directed and negotiated sales and marketing programs for the Southland 7-Eleven chain.
- Successfully obtained agreement on performance requirements that maximized company return on marketing investment.
National Sales Manager, Institutional Market
- Developed and implemented a successful test program of bottle and can products for the McDonald's and Burger King accounts.
- Directed the conversion of A.R.A.'s major vending facilities nationwide.

Lotsa-Cola U.S.A., Food Service Division, Chicago, Illinois, 1985 to 1990
National Key Account Manager
- Oversaw sales, distribution, and marketing development for five national accounts.
- Negotiated total K-Mart soft drink program including lease equipment agreements, customized menu board/merchandising programs, and trade and marketing allowance incentives.

Hunt-Wesson Foods, Inc., Atlanta, Georgia, 1984 to 1985
National Accounts Manager, Southern Region
- Responsible for institutional chain sales and distribution development for a 13-state region.

EDUCATION
George Washington University, Washington, D.C. • Bachelor of Arts, 1983
Columbia University, New York, NY • Graduate work in business

REFERENCES AVAILABLE

JASON WOO

345 Newell Drive • Kansas City, MO 56777 • (675) 555-6787 •
jason.woo@xxx.com

OBJECTIVE

Seeking an opportunity to utilize my extensive experience with a
company that offers growth and increasing responsibility.

SUMMARY OF BACKGROUND

Highly experienced in industrial painting applications and
management of complex organizations.

LAMAS INDUSTRIAL PAINTING

Warehouse Manager, 1999 to present

- Supervised efficient operation of a 35,000–square-foot industrial
  painting warehouse.
- Implemented a state-of-the-art tracing system to identify the
  exact location of shipments on a timely basis.
- Set up an inventory control system that was later profiled in
  industry trade journals as "the best example of a modernized
  system currently in operation."
- Negotiated a cost-saving labor agreement with the International
  Brotherhood of Manufacturing Workers.
- Utilized contract administrative-support personnel to meet
  unanticipated heavy-volume peak period, thus reducing benefit
  obligations and other costs.
- Identified trends in material handling, which were sequentially
  incorporated into the overall warehousing strategy.
- Fostered an environment of teamwork and high morale through
  implementation of self-directed teams.
- Modernized warehouse operation through purchase of robotic
  equipment used for mixing industrial paint supplies.
- Initiated an easily accessible order system that improved relationships between sales and manufacturing personnel and increased
  overall company sales.

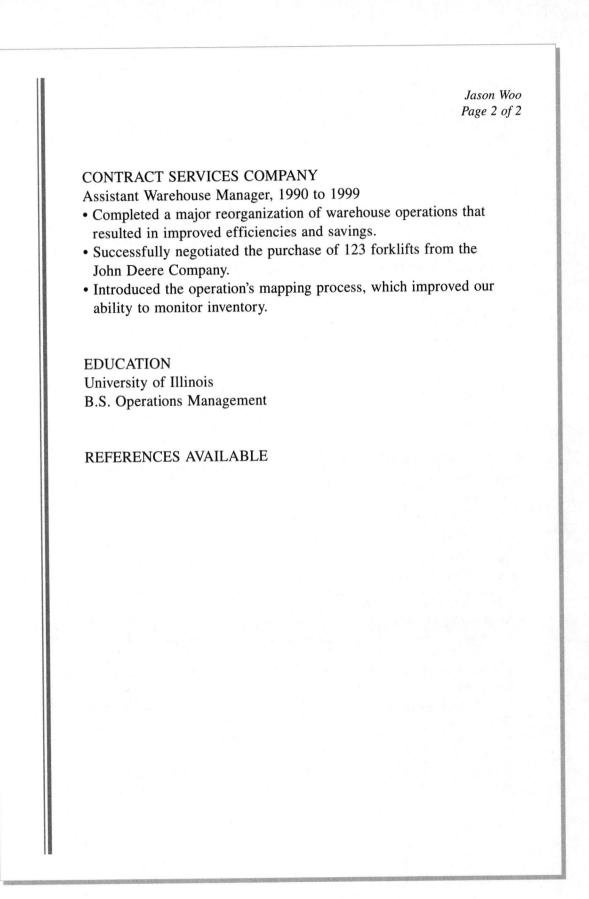

CONTRACT SERVICES COMPANY
Assistant Warehouse Manager, 1990 to 1999
- Completed a major reorganization of warehouse operations that resulted in improved efficiencies and savings.
- Successfully negotiated the purchase of 123 forklifts from the John Deere Company.
- Introduced the operation's mapping process, which improved our ability to monitor inventory.

EDUCATION
University of Illinois
B.S. Operations Management

REFERENCES AVAILABLE

Terry Edwardo

123 Center Lane   706-555-7865
Bartlesville, OK 74006   terryedwardo@xxx.com

Background Summary

Consumer packaged-goods executive with considerable experience in both domestic and international marketing and general management. Strengths in developing new products and new markets with proven capability to identify business opportunities, structure organizations, launch new products, and implement business plans. Effective in both line and staff roles in large corporate settings and in small entrepreneurial organizations with P&L responsibility.

Skilled in:

- Strategic business planning
- New product development
- Market prospecting
- New product introduction
- Contract negotiations
- International business

Professional Experience

Archway Brands, Tulsa, OK
1987–Present

Director, New Business Development
2002–Present

Report to the President of Archway Systems, a new venture unit. Responsible for the creation, development, and evaluation of a new soft-drink business system in the U.S., Germany, and Japan. Control an initial $10 million development program.

- Directed a team of engineers, marketing managers, market researchers, and graphic designers in Germany, Japan, and the U.S. in the development of a high-quality vending machine with consumer appeal.
- Initiated consumer and distribution system studies in the U.S. and Germany that resulted in establishing concept acceptance, market penetration levels, and distribution costs.
- Created a U.S. strategic business plan with a $35 million incremental profit potential in its fifth year.
- Negotiated $20 million joint appliance-development contract with a leading German vending appliance division.
- Developed a new policy for handling and analyzing third-party concept submissions that reduced evaluation periods and costs.

Professional Experience (continued)

Division Manager of Refrigerated Products, 2000–2002

Reported to Senior Vice President and Assistant to the President. Responsible for developing business plans for introduction of products in Japan. Annual turnover estimated at $25 million; long-term potential of $150 million.

- Developed strategic product position that was subsequently supported by consumer evaluation. Prepared television advertising and packaging graphics that supported the overall advertising objective.
- Identified a regional refrigerated distribution system for the introduction of new product rollout.
- Negotiated a third-party manufacturing contract and the purchase of additional import-restricted raw materials.

Director, Business Development, 1996–2000

Responsible for market development of core products.

- Analyzed worldwide business opportunities for expanding the business with particular emphasis on Europe, Latin America, and the Pacific Rim.
- Developed and launched a new business of exporting products from Brazil to North America and Europe.

Manager, Product Development, 1987–1996

Managed new-product development activities.

- Responsible for developing and launching numerous products from test market to regional rollout.
- Identified a new packaging system that resulted in our entering the market first.

Blue's Foods

1980–1987

Research Supervisor

Responsible for product development and improvement.

- Developed banana-flavored line of fruit drinks that resulted in market success.

Education

Pennsylvania State University, 1980

B.S., Biology

References available upon request.

OSCAR LAWRENCE JAKHI

3370 Barnaby Road • Lokalulu, GA 30222

Home: 404-555-7823 • Cell: 404-555-6634 • Oscar-Jakhi@xxx.com

---

EDUCATION

Mercer University, Atlanta, GA
Master of Business Administration, Concentration in Marketing
June 1990

George Washington University, Washington, D.C.
Bachelor of Arts in History
December 1986

ACADEMIC HIGHLIGHTS

- Analyzed Babson Company international expansion into the dry foods category.
- Developed a demand strategy and advertising plan.
- Conducted an extensive review of the leading competitive brands.
- Researched and recommended a pricing strategy for Colombian Coffee Mate brand.
- Analyzed the role of pricing on market share.
- Investigated cannibalization issues pertaining to a new product launch by Noruce Inc.
- Developed a strategy to position Noruce's Gold as a premium-priced product.

EXPERIENCE

Belgian-American Chamber of Commerce
- Coordinated marketing activities designed to increase ties between the Belgian trade mission and southeast businesses. 1998 to present

U.S. Department of Commerce
- Provided information on marketing and promotional activities to corporations seeking expansion into Europe. 1992 to 1998

REFERENCES

Available upon request.

SARAH JENNINGS

12 Barkley Place • Chicago, Illinois 60652 • (773) 555-2114 • sarahjennings@xxx.com

OBJECTIVE

A position in retailing

EXPERIENCE

Lendman's Department Stores, 1999 to present

1986 to present • Assistant Manager, Home Furnishings

• Responsible for sales, merchandising, and customer service.

• Assist customers in selecting home furnishings to meet their personal needs.

• Supervise a staff of seven sales assistants and merchandise clerks.

• Provide customer feedback to the corporate buying department and assist in the selection of new items.

1999 to 2006 • Sales Clerk, Home Furnishings

• Twice selected "Employee of the Month."

• Increased sales by 7 percent while reducing customer complaints by 30 percent.

• Selected to participate on a task force designed to improve selection and customer service in the home furnishings area.

1981 to 1999 • Homemaker

• Raised three children and held leadership positions in a variety of civic organizations.

• Active in the Chicago area YWCA, United Way Campaign, and other charitable causes.

• Served as United Way Membership Chairperson in 1995.

• Received a mayoral citation for excellent service.

1978 to 1981 • Sales Clerk, Women's Clothing, Yauckey's Department Stores

• Assisted customers in selection and clothing sales.

• Supervised junior sales clerks.

• Handled timecards and dispersing checks for owner.

References available upon request.

✦ Yonin Hussan

111 El Camino Real

Baltimore, MD 44444

(609) 555-7777

yonin.hussan@xxx.com

✦ Objective
A marketing or sales position in the chemical industry.

✦ Experience
Prime Chemicals, Baltimore, MD   *1970–Present*
Marketing Manager   1996–Present
- Increased sales 56 percent through the development of small and medium companies that were not previously cost-effective.
- Designated project leader of a team to evaluate direct mail as a means of increasing sales. Our recommendations to test the concept in a five-state region were approved and implemented by senior management.
- Reduced sales expenses by 11 percent through aggressive account management and innovative cost-control methods.

Midwestern Sales Representative   1983–1996
- Assigned as the first sales representative to market a specialty chemical line in the Midwest.
- Developed an initial marketing plan that targeted companies in the construction and home improvement industries.
- Consistently achieved 150 percent of quota.
- Winner of the "Golden Baton" award for sales excellence.

Sales Representative 1978–1983
- Increased sales by 46 percent and opened 159 new accounts.
- Gained recognition from senior management for developing the Tasty Lucky account of convenience stores.

✦ Education
Wayland High School, Honors Graduate 1978
Elected vice president of the senior class.

References available upon request.

JOHN F. COMMODY

1755 Tartan Springs Trail • Homer, GA 30077 • 404-555-6478 • johncommody@xxx.com

EXPERIENCE

2000 to Present • Plants Etc. Inc., Atlanta, GA
General Manager and Chief Operating Officer
- Recruited to provide turnaround management expertise to a leading specialty corporation involved in the manufacturing, wholesaling, and retailing of silk botanicals. Specific focus was on redefining the strategic direction of the retail operations.
- Developed a major market strategy focused on consolidating activities. Increased market penetration in the southeast. Opened three new retail stores in the Atlanta area while substantially reducing financial losses.
- Recruited marketing, finance, and warehousing staff. Hired and trained additional sales representatives to increase service levels to wholesale clients.
- Implemented accounting procedures including a perpetual inventory system.

1980 to 2000 • Read Drug Company, Subsidiary of Edwards Drug Stores, Atlanta, GA
Senior Divisional Vice President and Chief Operating Officer • 1993 to 2000
- Overall general management responsibility for 90 stores employing 1,200 people, producing $120 million in annual retail sales.
- Supervised Vice Presidents of Operations, Marketing, Warehousing, and Professional Services.
- Developed merchandising, acquisition, divestiture, and expansion strategies.
- Developed budget projections and pro formas on new locations. Directed the closing of seven existing stores and the opening of 16 new facilities.
- Implemented an extensive remodeling and merchandising program for all company units. Activities resulted in an average 18 percent increase in store sales.

Regional Vice President, Store Operations • 1985 to 1993
- Responsible for 70 retail stores with annual sales of $90 million in the Baltimore, Northern Maryland, and southern Pennsylvania region.
- Integrated acquisition into the Edwards organization.

District Manager • 1980 to 1985
- Responsible for all transition issues and the introduction of Edwards store format and retailing methods. Developed and initiated district promotions and advertising, and directed local buying activity.

EDUCATION

University of Baltimore, Baltimore, MD
- 1979, Bachelor of Science: Marketing/Management
- Minor: Accounting
- Additional postgraduate work in business administration.

ASSOCIATIONS

Director, March of Dimes, Richmond, VA

REFERENCES AVAILABLE UPON REQUEST

JAFTA SUMA
123 Gorden Street • Phoenix, AZ 23432
607-555-6789 • jaftasuma@xxx.com

Summary
Highly experienced in the development and management of document imaging systems.

Experience
Sales Manager, 1995 to Present • Morgan Software Company
- Generated a 45 percent increase in sales through the development and implementation of innovative marketing strategies.
- Hired and mentored sales associates, reducing turnover by 26 percent.
- Identified an important new business market for the company that resulted in increased sales and profitability.
- Fostered an environment of mutual support by developing a company mission and values statement.
- Modernized the customer support organization by upgrading the telephone system and providing training on effective customer-service techniques.
- Initiated a guarantee program that was the first in our industry. Based on the success of the program, the company received a distinguished service award from the Microfilm Manufacturers Association.
- Identified nonperforming product areas and developed recommendations for their discontinuation.
- Edited a technical training manual that was used extensively throughout the company.

Sales Manager, 1984 to 1995 • IMS-Imaging Services
- Originally hired as a territory sales trainee; promoted into management based on superior performance.
- Implemented a new product drive that opened up new markets for the company.
- Elected by industry peers to judge the "Best of Show" awards in Atlantic City.
- Modernized the cobalt imaging system to include the hydrogen confluence line of products, which resulted in a 65 percent increase in company sales.

Education
B.S. Computer Science, University of Maine, Orono, ME
A.A. Computer Science, Eastern Maine Community College, Bangor, ME

References
Available upon request

JASON LOCKLY
1160 Sunnyside Place • Boston, MA 01773
(617) 555-3343 • lockly@xxx.com

CAREER SUMMARY
Twenty-eight years of progressive experience in human resources, management, and financial activities in both a large, professional business environment and a small start-up operation. A team-oriented, client-service-driven, and cost-efficient manager.

EXPERIENCE
Richard S. James Associates
Managing Director, 1993–Present
- Responsible for opening the Boston office of a full-service financial recruiting organization. Office has grown to a staff of eight with billings of $1.7 million.
- Successfully marketed the firm's services to companies in the metropolitan Boston area.
- Increased revenue growth 27 percent despite poor economic conditions for corporate hiring.
- Managed a staff of seven with responsibility for overall office management.

Price Waterhouse, Boston
Director of Human Resources, 1990–1993
- Responsible for overall coordination of human resources activities for a 24-office region. Initiated a national recruiting program at eight MBA schools.
- Planned and conducted annual training meetings for recruiters, including basic interview skills workshops.
- Earlier positions with Price Waterhouse included Executive Recruitment Manager, Practice Development Manager, and Audit Senior Staff Accountant.

United States Navy
Supply Corps Officer, 1981–1989

EDUCATION
Ohio University, Athens, OH
B.A. 1979, Business Administration

References available upon request.

VINCENZO LAPENA

87 Bradley Drive

Dallas, TX 87665

Home: (908) 555-8722

Cell: (908) 555-8722

Email: lapena@xxx.com

EXPERIENCE

Southwestern Telecom Inc.
Purchasing Commodity Manager, 1996–present

Responsible for negotiating contract service agreements and the procurement of MRO, capital equipment, and inventory commodities. Annual buying group responsibility of $22,000,000. Personally responsible for $11,000,000 in annual purchases. Senior Buyer for six years prior to current position, which reports to the Director of Purchasing. Accomplished the following:

- Generated cost improvements in excess of $2,000,000 annually.

- Analyzed RFQs and awarded contract purchase agreements.

- Acted as the region's Contract Administrator responsible for maintaining and communicating internally all local and national purchasing contract agreements.

- Developed a supplier stocking program reducing inventory levels by 75 percent.

- Supported and met corporate goals in doing business with women-owned, minority, and small business suppliers.

- Coordinated the implementation of computerized expense purchasing.

- Maintained on-time delivery performance exceeding 95 percent.

Hadlock Inns of America
Purchasing Agent, 1978–1996

Responsible for the procurement of products and services for all properties throughout the United States.

EDUCATION

Aquinas College, Grand Rapids, MI

B.S. Mathematics, 1976

Graduated in top 10 percent of class

REFERENCES AVAILABLE

SAM ANDREWS

224 Field Street • Jackson, MI 64332 • (621) 555-9087 • samandrews@xxx.com

- -

Profile

Self-starter with excellent planning and organizational skills in Human Resources Management

Education

B.A., Business, 1982
Michigan State University, Lansing, MI

Experience

Contract Benefits Administrator
Concraco World Headquarters
1986–present
• Responsible for the administration of pension and flexible benefits programs for all chemical plants throughout the United States.
• Designed and implemented salary and wage administration policies and procedures.
• Conducted management seminars regarding labor laws and recent legislation.
• Held executive board presentations on all benefit and compensation proposals.
• Outlined a comprehensive wellness program in conjunction with the American Cancer Society.
• Administered affirmative action policies and procedures and filed annual EEO reports.

Compensation Specialist
St. Mary's Hospital
1982–1986
• Administered a variety of compensation, unemployment, garnishment, and employee relations policies and procedures.
• Implemented employee incentive budgets and planned annual employee recognition events.
• Generated more than $50,000 in annual human resources–sponsored fundraisers.
• Supervised clerical support and volunteer department staff.

References Available

John E. Carlson

58862 Mill Road • Boat Head, IN 55555 • (612) 555-7266 Residence
(612) 555-3462 Office • johncarlson@xxx.com

2005–Present:
Independent Consultant

- Write, lecture, and consult on human resources and industrial relations.
- Clients include Fortune 500 corporations, trade associations, and universities.

1990–2005:
Fresh Foods, Inc., Chicago, IL
Director of Human Resources

- Senior human resources officer for the $2.2 billion grocery division. Particular emphasis on management development, employee selection, and succession planning.
- Introduced management training and education programs on strategic business planning, selection decision making, and performance appraisal.
- Analyzed acquisition candidates as a member of the due diligence team.

Manager, Recruiting and Staffing

- Recruited to Fresh Foods to establish a coordinated staffing department.
- Directed the development of an overall recruiting strategy.
- Designed and implemented initial M.B.A. recruiting program.
- Initiated a highly successful Junior Military Officer recruiting program.
- Established credibility for the recruiting function with senior-level line managers and operating heads.

1979–1990:
Restaurant Products, Inc.
Manager, Corporate Employment

- Recruited managerial, professional, and technical positions for overall headquarters.
- Designed and implemented initial college-relations program.

B.A. English, Washington University, St. Louis, MO
M.A. Career Development, Norwich University, Northfield, VT

References available upon request.

CARLOS VASQUEZ

5431 Clinchfield Trail • Austin, TX 32445
607-555-8877 • Carlos-Vasquez@xxx.com

PROFESSIONAL EXPERIENCE

Major Account Representative, Arrow Shirt Co.	2003–Present
Sales Representative, Arrow Shirt Co.	1992–2003
Associate Sales Representative, Arrow Shirt Co.	1980–1992
Sales Manager, Bulldog Movers	1969–1980
Sales Representative, A. B. Dick Co.	1968–1969

PROFESSIONAL HIGHLIGHTS

- Responsible for key account activity for 45 branch stores and 60 specialty shops with sales volume of $3 million.
- Introduced innovative sales and promotional programs to maintain market share in an eroding business environment.
- Increased sales by $200,000 through the introduction of a promotion targeted to the spring sales items.
- Overcame buyer reluctance stemming from competitive pricing issues through the introduction of a private-label program.
- Successfully increased market share by 70 percent by successfully introducing dress shirt and sportswear lines.
- Directed the marketing and sales activities for a start-up transportation company.
- Promoted three times in five years.
- Maintained inventories to ensure proper levels of merchandise throughout the selling season.

EDUCATION

Completed two years' university work at the University of Texas.

References available upon request

ROBIN WHITE

2431 Caves Road • Owings Mills, MD 21165
Home: (410) 555-7302 • Cell: (410) 555-6621
Email: robinwhite@xxx.com

PROFILE

Results-oriented senior human resources professional with diverse industry experience. Skilled in building customer-driven teams that contribute to successful organizational performance. Recognized leadership, interpersonal, problem-solving, and conceptual strengths. Energetic change agent and strategic business partner in working with people at all levels to launch new initiatives.

Demonstrated expertise in:
• Recruitment and selection
• Management development
• Turnover reduction
• Succession planning
• Quality improvement
• Compensation management
• Benefit cost control
• EEOC and legal compliance

PROFESSIONAL EXPERIENCE

Consumer Bank, Laurel, MD   1978 to present
Vice President, Human Resources   1997 to present

Established and developed the human resources division for a $3 billion bank holding company and subsidiaries with 2,000 employees and 120 branches in three states. Report to the president of the holding company. Recruit professional staff and direct all human resources activities.

PROFESSIONAL EXPERIENCE (continued)

Achievements also included:

- Contributed to the bank's increase in market share and deposit growth by installing service quality (TQM) program, resulting in the bank's rise from last to first place in customer satisfaction ratings.
- Implemented new recruiting and selection programs and procedures, resulting in savings of more than $100,000 annually.
- Introduced managed-care program to control self-insured health care costs and retain high-quality coverage.
- Saved corporation $1 million by resolving class-action lawsuit with EEOC.

References available upon request

YUKI MIZAGUCHI

2 Elm Street
Boston, MA 01773
617-555-3456
Yuki.Mizaguchi@xxx.com

SUMMARY

More than 30 years of executive leadership experience in a large and expanding national organization. A high-energy, intuitive manager and organizational architect with powerful analytical skills and the proven ability to achieve long-term, bottom-line results through strong marketing and management orientation. Commitment to effective team building and sound client relations.

Management and Strategic Planning
Designed and directed a merger with a sister company, totaling 750 staff and 22 offices, that resulted in a 20 percent reduction in overhead costs. Reduced staff costs, maximized staff productivity, and improved morale and stability.

Strategic Planning and Marketing
Designed and implemented a structure to provide for concentrated marketing to targeted clients, resulting in increased immediate and long-term revenues.

EXPERIENCE

Walters Engineering, Boston, MA
President, 1998 to present

Lamont Heavy Industries, St. Louis, MO
Regional Vice President, 1988 to 1998

Maine Department of Public Works, Bangor, ME
Engineer, 1981 to 1988

EDUCATION

B.S., Civil Engineering
University of Maine, Bangor, ME

REFERENCES

Available upon request

ROBERT HEFF

2 Ridway Lane • Windsor, CT 08976

Robert_Heff@xxx.com • 203-555-9637

THE BUFFALO GROUP

Established and organized this corporation to import and distribute national writing instruments by Jockensteem of Germany. Purchased assets of manufacturer's existing subsidiary. Sales were made through conventional retail channels and to advertising specialty distributors.

President and Owner, 1996–2008

Doubled sales to $1 million in first year of operation. Reached breakeven in profit. Created new company identification, national advertising, and catalogs. Completely computerized operation to provide instant customer service and financial reports. Set up manufacturer representative organization for retail sales while improving performance of ad specialty representatives. Added new product enhancement that resulted in company's largest sale. Sold operation as an ongoing business.

BENNINGTON CORPORATION OF AMERICA

This $300 million subsidiary of Bennington of London manufactures and distributes consumer and industrial electronic products in the United States.

Assistant Vice President, Marketing, 1991–1996

Responsible for marketing services, personnel, real estate, purchasing, and a hi-fi speaker plant. Supervised design and construction of a national service and parts center in St. Louis. Returned speaker plant to profitability on sales of $4 million.

ACME TYPEWRITER COMPANY

This $100 million subsidiary manufactured and sold office typewriters, portable typewriters, copiers, word processing equipment, and electronic calculators wholesale and direct through retail branches.

Vice President, Administration, 1989–1991

Responsible for computer operations, product and spare parts distribution, personnel, purchasing, and export administration. Budget $6.4 million; head count 192; reported to the president.

Product Manager for Consumer Products, 1980–1989

Responsible for formulation of business plans for each new consumer product. Coordinated all company efforts leading to new product introductions.

References available upon request.

ROBERT CHEKOV
522 Market Street, Lewisburg, PA 17837   Home: (709) 555-8877
Email: robertchekov@xxx.com   Cell: (709) 555-7115

SUMMARY
- More than thirty years of progressive management and marketing experience within demanding business environments.
- Proven ability to assess organizational need and implement effective administrative procedures.
- Multilingual; experienced communicating with varied cultures and all levels within an organization.
- Proficient at working independently, handling simultaneous projects, and meeting deadlines.
- Strong management, problem-solving, and supervisory skills.

ACCOMPLISHMENTS
- Provided technical and advisory support to manufacturing plants.
- Participated in alternate supplier approvals.
- Increased departmental output by 50 percent.
- Developed and implemented a new format for ingredient specifications.
- Doubled projected sales volume for an international office supply firm.
- Directed all business activities for a highly profitable textile manufacturing organization.
- Devised innovative and highly efficient methods of optimizing raw materials.
- Increased net profits from 12 percent to 35 percent, and increased productivity of manufactured products by 40 percent.

EMPLOYMENT

Specifications Technologist	American Home Products	1985 to present
Division Manager	SP Clobus/SP Coopprom	1979 to 1984
Sales Broker	Sales Distribution Co.	1978 to 1979
Medical Support	Bulgarian Armed Forces	1976 to 1978

EDUCATION

M.S. International Business, Bucknell University, Lewisburg, PA   1980
B.S., Higher Medical Institute of Pleven, Medical Academy, Bulgaria   1968

LANGUAGES
Fluent in English, German, Bulgarian
Conversant in Russian and Macedonian

REFERENCES AVAILABLE ON REQUEST

ROB PETRY
21 Elm Road
Cranston, RI 45677
401-555-6118
robpetry@xxx.com

OBJECTIVE
Seeking a position as a draftsman or architectural designer in a commercial architectural firm.

EXPERIENCE
Brady, Sorrel & Johnson Architects
Draftsman, 2005 to present
• Assisted in developing plans for multiple residential and commercial projects.

Cooley Construction Company
Assistant Shift Supervisor, 2000 to 2005
• Managed the activities of up to six plumbers and bricklayers.
• Responsible for interviewing new employees, administering payroll, and tracking inventory.

Ritchie Construction Company
Master Carpenter, 1985 to 2000
• Progressed as an apprentice from carpenter's assistant to master's level.
• Assisted in the reconstruction of the famed Warwick Musical Theater, Warwick, RI.

TRAINING
• Drafting School, New Rochelle, NY
Vocational and Technical Center, 2005
• Completed ten months of training in night school program.

EDUCATION
Graduate of Laura Dancer High School

ADDITIONAL INFORMATION
Open to relocation
Skilled in all relevant computer programs

REFERENCES AVAILABLE UPON REQUEST

KATHERINE MORIETI

123 Wayland Road
Seattle, WA 76666
kmorieti@xxx.com
(555) 540-7005

OBJECTIVE

Position as a registered nurse

EDUCATION AND CERTIFICATION

A.A. Nursing
University of Washington, Tacoma, WA, 1972

B.A. Nursing
University of Washington, Tacoma, WA, 1981
Registered Dietician certification, 1982
Certified Occupational Therapist, 2001

EXPERIENCE

Registered Nurse experienced in

- Intensive care
- Surgery
- Post-operative care
- Hospital administration

Page 1 of 2

EMPLOYMENT

Northwest Hospital, Seattle, WA	2002–present
Saint Peter Hospital, Olympia, WA	1997–2002
Mirabella Retirement Center, Seattle, WA	1995–1997
St. Mary's Hospital, Walla Walla, WA	1985–1995
Deaconness Center, Spokane, WA	1981–1985
Allenmore Hospital, Tacoma, WA	1972–1981

ADDITIONAL ACTIVITIES

Chess, reading, horseshoes, calligraphy

REFERENCES

Available upon request

YOLANDA WILLIAMS

12 Peachtree Industrial Rd.
Atlanta, GA 30338
404-555-6666
Y.E.Williams@xxx.com

JOB OBJECTIVE

Systems Software Designer, Applications Engineer

EDUCATION

B.S. Information and Computer Science, 2005
University of Georgia, Athens, GA

B.A. History, 1984
Emory University, Atlanta, GA

GENERAL BACKGROUND

Following a successful 17-year career in education, I returned to school
to complete an undergraduate degree in computer science. My experience
is in software design and testing for various processors and real-time
systems.

SPECIFIC EXPERIENCE

2005–Present
National Systems Corporation, Atlanta, GA
Systems Engineer
• Develop division plans, guidelines, and policies for the use and
  acquisition of software and hardware for the division. Participate on
  the committee for implementation of policies on the corporate level.
  Evaluate and select software and hardware for purchase. Represent
  the company at conferences and user groups.

SPECIFIC EXPERIENCE (continued)

- Design team member in the development of control software. Employed structured design techniques and methodologies.
- Directed the development of tracker software, monitor, diagnostics, test software, and documentation.
- Conducted analysis for general-purpose imaging processing hardware, including infrared search, track imaging, target segmentation, and tracker applications.

1984–2001
Druid Hills High School, Atlanta, GA
History Teacher/Assistant Principal

References available upon request.

Marshall Solomon

1209 Brakeman Court
Albany, WI 65443
(802) 555-9873
Cell: (802) 555-2332
marshallsolomon@xxx.com

Objective

Materials acquisition or marketing services position that would utilize my extensive experience in these fields.

Qualifications

More than 35 years of experience in materials acquisition, including 20 years in supervision and 15 years in contract development and administration. Provided direct support to sales, marketing, and legal departments in all areas of product development and introduction.

Results-oriented manager with excellent skills in:

- contract negotiation
- problem solving
- budgeting and forecasting
- time management
- cost-reduction
- recruitment and training

Education

M.B.A., Southern Illinois University, Carbondale, IL, 1978
B.S., Tennessee State University, Nashville, TN, 1975

Professional Experience

Mustang Cola, 1981–Present, Senior Marketing Materials Buyer

- Manage the procurement and development of division's permanent merchandising and marketing display materials.
- Directly responsible for managing departmental operating budget totaling $2.5 million in point-of-sale material expenditures.
- Successfully developed a point-of-sale marketing program that generated $275,000 for the division's annual operating budget.

Douglas Gant Inc., 1978–1981, Senior Analyst

- Negotiated and administered commercial and governmental contracts for the sale and licensing of materials and hardware supplies. Total contractual responsibilities exceeded $50 million annually.
- Issued contracts for the licensing of proprietary and custom third-party materials. Successfully represented the company in complex negotiations.

References available on request

Rob Stevowski · 215 East Stone Drive · Kingsport, Tennessee 37660
(615) 555-1212 · (615) 555-5223 · robstevowski@xxx.com

Education

University of Cincinnati, Cincinnati, OH, 1973
Master of Business Administration in Finance

Bowling Green State University, Bowling Green, OH, 1972
Bachelor of Science in Accounting

Experience

1994 to present · Miller Graphics, Kingsport, Tennessee
Group Manager: Financial Analysis/Marketing and Cost

- Responsible for the development and coordination of pricing policies and procedures for a five-state division with $550 million in sales.
- Responsible for the preparation of marketing competitive analysis.
- Supervised the efforts of six direct reports.
- Responsible for the development of the marketing segment of the annual business plan and long-range business forecast.

Additional responsibilities as of 2005:

- Responsible for the coordination of the cost accounting activities for the five-division group. This includes standards maintenance, variance reporting, and financial systems maintenance.
- Responsible for the development and execution of the group's inventory reduction program.
- Standardized the methodology necessary to compute divisional financial burden rates.
- Reviewed and analyzed divisional requests for capital expenditures.

1981 to 1994 · Epstein/Sexton Corporation, Holland, Michigan
Manager: Financial Operations

- Responsible for cost accounting, profit planning, budgeting, accounts payable, accounts receivable, payroll, and cash management functions for this $12 million company.

1978 to 1981 · Jackson, Bennett & Smith, Certified Public Accountants
Staff Accountant

- Joined this regional accounting firm after completion of M.B.A. Audited clients in the food and hospitality industries.

References available on request

SONJA GRISWALD

2732 Greenridge Rd.

Tulsa, OK 66777

515-555-1212 • Sonja_Griswald@xxx.com

Objective

To obtain a senior-level sales position in the insurance industry.

Experience

2004–Present
Biltmore Insurance Group
Senior Sales Representative
- Responsible for selling $300,000 contracts to individuals and small businesses in a four-state southeastern sales territory.
- Increased personal production by 35 percent over the past two years.
- Developed a marketing program that resulted in a 93 percent conversion rate.
- Implemented a direct-mail program to attract employee payroll deduction participation.

1992–2004
Universal Insurance
Sales Representative
- Increased sales 75 percent in five years.
- Twice awarded salesman of the month.

1977–1994
Tulsa School District #43
Teacher/Coach
- Taught science and mathematics in grades K–8.
- Coached girls' soccer and gymnastics.

References

Available upon request.

Diego Lopez

45 Marshfield Lane
El Segundo, CA 98766
310-555-8764
Diego.Lopez@xxx.com

Objective

A research, data analysis, or administrative position that will use my
leadership and organizational skills.

Education

A.A. El Segundo Community College, 1983
Major: Administration
G.P.A. 3.87/4.0

Strengths

Leadership

- Organized the annual United Way company drive.
- Achieved record-setting results.
- Elected chairperson of the El Segundo PTA.
- Delegated tasks to Commerce volunteers.

Responsibility

- Assisted in the implementation of a companywide word-processing
  system.
- Handled confidential information, materials, and files for the director of
  human resources.
- Input personal information and updated databases.
- Handled all office procurement and distributing orders.
- Answered phones and directed calls to appropriate department.

Organization
- Revised the filing system to track applicants applying to the company.
- Created a new computerized system to monitor administrative expenses.
- Developed a database of all current and past donors.

Experience

1995–present
Jurassic Petroleum Company
Administrative assistant to the director of human resources

1991–1995
El Segundo Chamber of Commerce
Front Desk/Office Manager

1983–1991
Jefferson Autobody
Front Desk/Customer Service

References provided upon request.

KAMIR ALUWAND

76 Reedy Drive
Louisville, KY 33454
(876) 555-6785
Kamir_Aluwand@xxx.com

OBJECTIVE

A senior-level accounting or financial position.

EXPERIENCE

Controller, Transpack Industries, 1985–Present
- Responsible for all accounting and financial functions for this $4.5 million manufacturer of packaging materials.
- Monitored cash disbursements to the sales force for compliance purposes.
- Implemented an automated cash-flow analysis system, which resulted in the saving of $53,000 for the company.
- Launched an initiative to lobby legislators and other elected officials to lower the capital gains tax on certain company transactions.

Elected President of the Louisville Society of CPAs, 2004–Present
- Projected cash-flow needs based on actual and anticipated receivables and billings.
- Reorganized the accounting department to make it more responsive to line management needs for accurate and timely financial service.

EDUCATION

University of Georgia, Athens, GA
Master of Business Administration

University of Louisville, Louisville, KY
B.S. Accounting

- Passed CPA exam in first sitting
- Licensed and registered CPA in Kentucky and Georgia

References available upon request.

John Laviachech

1343 Flower Street

Garden Grove, CA 92643

(714) 555-0987

J_Laviachech@xxx.com

Objective

To continue my successful career in the chemical industry

Education

B.S., Chemistry, August 1975
University of California—Los Angeles

Areas of Continuing Education
- Digital and analog chemical analysis
- Systems and signal
- Signal processing
- Probability and statistics
- Semi-fluid devices
- Feedback field and wave control

Special Skills

Experience with developing heat and material balances and process flow diagrams (PFDs), piping and instrument drawings (P&IDs), and various unit operations and equipment (including distillation columns, heat exchangers, and pumps)

Experience

Chemist, University of California—Los Angeles, 1986 to present
Designed and analyzed chemical reactions in slurry-bed reactors and chemical bed systems.

Laboratory Technician, Simpson Kerr Chemicals, 1975 to 1986
Tested samples of dental chemical materials during each phase of the process.

Chemistry Tutor, UCLA, 1974
Assisted freshman and sophomore students studying the basics of chemistry.

References Available

Frank Sabatini

111 Piada Drive

Miami, FL 34567

(813) 555-7878

Frank_Sabatini@xxx.com

Extensive general management experience in pharmaceutical and consumer industries.

Employment History

Jackson Pharmaceuticals, Miami, FL

1996–present

General Manager, Marketing and Sales

• Launched a new-product introduction achieving sales of $5 million in six months.

• Directed a divestment strategy in several states to avoid $2.5 million in losses.

• Reduced inventories and accounts receivable to minimize high-interest costs.

• Appointed new management team in Florida. Profitability was restored from a loss of $1.3 million to a profit of $250,000.

Bentley Products, Phoenix, AZ

1985–1996

Sales Manager, New Products

• Developed new-products strategy and identified new business opportunities.

• Increased sales from $100,000 in 1985 to $2.1 million in 1996.

Education

B.A., Business, University of Detroit, Detroit, MI

Additional Skills

Experienced in using Microsoft Office and Microsoft Access.

References Available On Request.

Janet Johnomile

2 Cabot Drive • Wichita, Kansas 67202

janetjohnomile@xxx.com • Cell: (308) 555-6114 • Home: (308) 555-7812

Alexander & Robinson, 1992 to present

Executive Administrative Assistant to the Vice President of Human Resources

• Assist the Vice President in managing training and development, succession planning, and human resources regulatory compliance for this insurance brokerage firm with more than $1 billion in sales and 8,000 U.S. employees.

• Organized and led administrative training team to identify and support diversity requirements.

• Coordinated the administrative introduction of management development programs, dramatically improving managerial skills and employee relations.

• Assisted in the implementation of a formalized succession-planning program to retain and develop high-potential performers.

Nugget Foods Corporation, 1982 to 1992

Senior Secretary to the Director of Human Resources

• Provided administrative and organizational support in the functional areas of staffing, training, and organizational development.

• Provided administrative leadership in the redesign and restaffing efforts of the marketing group.

• Coordinated administrative details for a senior-management task force to formulate corporate mission statement.

• Initiated a preventive health/wellness program for nonexempt employees as a long-range means of health-care cost containment.

• Provided support to a newly formed training and development function. Assisted in needs analyses and cost-effective programs tied to business objectives.

References available upon request.

HOROKO KIMURA

12 Boise St. • Jackson, IL 55555 • (756) 555-0987 • H.Kimura@xxx.com

OBJECTIVE

Senior financial or controller position with opportunity for advancement.

SUMMARY

Extensive financial experience across diverse product lines and markets. Comfortable dealing with complex organizations on a national scale. Unique combination of training in accounting, finance, and taxation. Vision and strong strategic-planning capabilities. Ability to create environment of achievement.

CAREER BACKGROUND

Lubbutt International, 1997 to present

Lubbutt is an international manufacturer of process control valves and computer-based control room instrumentation with turnkey engineering and installation capabilities. Sales total $750 million (two-thirds in the U.S.), with an asset base of $650 million supported by a workforce of 9,000 at 35 sites throughout the world.

Controller, 2004 to present

Responsibility worldwide for integrity of financial data, internal controls, proactive planning, and analysis. Responsibilities extend to each plant site and involve 370 individuals within the controllership function.

Accomplishments include:

• Managed worldwide breakeven analysis to assess severity of oil price–driven downturn. Restored profit through aggressive cost controls and adoption of early retirement plan in the U.S., England, and France.

• Coordinated domestic/foreign accounting, actuary, tax, and treasury expertise to ensure adoption of FASB 87 pension rules.

• Revised monthly financial reporting to more effectively link P&L with the balance sheet highlighting return of investment and cash-flow performance.

• Led implementation of worldwide consolidation system resulting in substantial EDP cost savings.

Page 1 of 2

CAREER BACKGROUND (continued)

Accounting Manager, 1997 to 2004

- Conducted review and approved changes in cost-allocation practices generating price and volume changes in custom versus standard products. Positive income impact approaching $3.3 million.

- Supervised rigorous capital budgeting reviews generating $6 million involving lease/buy alternatives, $8 million in government grant opportunities, and $1.2 million in additional investment tax credits.

Cook, Bartle & Stone

Senior Accountant, 1988 to 1997

- Accountant in the Washington, D.C., and Tampa offices. Concentration on audit and tax matters.

Earlier experience includes U.S. Army and positions in the textile industry.

EDUCATION/CERTIFICATION

University of Illinois, Springfield, IL
Bachelor of Science in Accounting

University of Illinois, Springfield, IL
Master of Business Administration

CPA: Illinois & Florida

REFERENCES

Available upon request.

CARMEN SANCHEZ

4 Walnut Creek Blvd. • Los Angeles, CA 30087
Home: 310-555-8733 • Cell: 310-555-5432 • Email: Carmen.Sanchez@xxx.com

OBJECTIVE

A position in public relations that involves planning and coordination between support groups and clients.

STRENGTHS AND SKILLS

PLANNING AND COORDINATING

Successfully directed the public relations efforts for a wide range of companies and industries. Managed an in-house committee to provide "real world" perspective to local area colleges. Designed an interactive instruction program for older students. Instructed creative writing at the primary and secondary grade levels.

MARKETING

Designed a successful promotions plan to attract new clients. Coordinated the media's coverage of our high-profile position in the St. Francis Day parade and picnic. Wrote several speeches for senior managers. Assisted in the development of public relations marketing materials.

COMMUNICATIVE SKILLS

Conducted more than 125 public presentations to local businesses and civic associations. Authored several articles promoting increased business involvement in civic activities. Significant experience as a writing instructor.

EDUCATION

B.A. University of California at Los Angeles, 1986
Major: English

EXPERIENCE

National Cinemedia–L.A .Office
May 2001–present

AOL Time Warner
January 1996–May 2001

Freelance Consulting
August 1986–January 1996
Various clients included Los Angeles Community College, L.A. Public Schools System, Dell Computers, Shriners Hospital, McDonald's, and Covina Chamber of Commerce.

References and a complete list of consulting clients available upon request.

YOSIF BHUTTO

123 West St. NW • Washington, D.C. 20002
(202) 555-7190 • yosif.bhutto@xxx.com

Objective
A professional sales, customer service, or administrative position with an opportunity to advance to management.

Education
B.A. in History, 1985 • George Washington University, Washington, D.C.
• Numerous courses in communications, psychology, and public speaking.
• Graduated in top 25 percent of class.

Experience
Jackson & Edwards • Administrative Assistant, 1994–present
• Responsible for all office management and purchasing for this Washington, D.C.–based management consulting firm.
• Improved the efficiency of office personnel by implementing a time-management training program.

Dobis Office Supplies • Customer Service Representative, 1988–1994
• Responsible for the development of communications programs between the company and its customers.
• Handled customer complaints.
• Received an "outstanding" performance review for five consecutive years.

Sears Roebuck & Co. • Sales Representative, Children's Toys, 1985–1988
• Reorganized product displays.
• Organized a 500-piece inventory.
• Created several successful sales promotions.

Additional Information
• Active in civic groups and the Chamber of Commerce.
• Enjoy reading, bridge, and traveling.

References
Available upon request.

E. Jane Hernandez

2100 Lakeland Marina Rd. #301F • Atlanta, GA 30131
(404) 555-3211 • (404) 555-9873 • janehernandez@xxx.com

1999–Present
Dawson Ltd., Atlanta, GA
Marketing Manager

Responsible for marketing research, product testing, and space planning for this owner and operator of upscale hotel and airline retail outlets. Serve as the key liaison between merchandising and operations. Direct marketing research strategies to determine areas and products for expansion.

Key Accomplishments: Successfully designed and implemented marketing analysis programs that recommended product expansions and new business targets. Developed an assortment analysis strategy that allocates space by category. Introduced a successful open-to-buy program for buyers. Initiated a product and pricing philosophy and strategy for buyers.

1990–1999
Tucul Inc., Atlanta, GA
Marketing Analyst

Directed the analysis of potential new business markets for this $15 million manufacturer of cellulosic films. Responsible for the development and analysis of monthly sales management reports and foreign competitive review.

Key Accomplishments: Initiated the analysis and development of price structures and 12-month import forecast. Provided leadership between the marketing and data-processing departments in the systems-driven marketing reports.

1980–1990
Fibers USA Inc., Atlanta, GA
Assistant Product Manager

Responsible for the identification, evaluation, and recommendation of new business opportunities. Monitored and evaluated market conditions and competitive activity for the nonwovens new-product development group. Responsible for five-year forecasts utilizing A.C. Nielsen data.

Key Accomplishments: Successfully coordinated the implementation of marketing strategies for several new business entries. Developed credibility with senior management by providing assessments on new business marketing opportunities.

1978–1980
M. Kessell & Associates, Knoxville, TN
Consulting Associate

Utilized secondary market research to investigate potential market opportunities for clients in diverse industries. Developed characteristic models on product markets. Conducted competitor-marketing analysis. Formulated demand analysis and recommended strategies and tactics to achieve marketing and corporate objectives. Developed a market-opportunity analysis for securing venture capital funding.

Masters of Business Administration
Concentrations in Marketing and Management
1980, University of Tennessee, Knoxville, TN

Bachelor of Arts in English
1977, University of Tennessee, Knoxville, TN

Systems Knowledge: Lotus Notes, MS Office, Crosstalk, Dialoglink, Dialog Electronic Databases, A.C. Nielsen Electronic Database, Symphony, Harvard Graphics, Windows XP.

References available upon request.

NORM BITWELL

29 Old Cumberland Trail • St. Louis, MO 63105

(314) 555-3476 • Cell: (314) 555-9833 • normbitwell@xxx.com

CAREER SUMMARY

Results-oriented senior scientist with practical and novel approaches to solving complex problems.

Extensive and Strong Skills in:
Chemical process development
Waste minimization and treatment
Technical support to manufacturing

ACCOMPLISHMENTS

CHEMICAL PROCESS DEVELOPMENT

• Developed solventless procedures for esterification of monomers, eliminating the need for solvent use and recovery.
• Developed procedures to remove tar-like sediment with dye compounds, thereby avoiding threatened shutdown of plant production.
• Pioneered single-vessel process for pigmentation, resulting in savings of $1 million in new equipment.
• Invented a procedure for recovery and reuse of complex photographic sheets using hot water.

WASTE MINIMIZATION AND TREATMENT

• Developed a process to dispose of large quantities of inorganic salts mixed with toxic organic solvents.
• Replaced carcinogenic solvents used in the manufacture of dye intermediates with safe and off-the-shelf reagents.
• Removed heavy polymer residues from polymerization vessels using mixed reagents.

TECHNICAL SUPPORT TO MANUFACTURING

• Applied creative techniques to salvage reject chemicals, resulting in $5 million in savings.
• Established that sensitive photographic emulsions could be manufactured in volume outside the laboratory with increased reliability and productivity.
• Modified multi-step synthesis of organic intermediates into single-vessel processes with one-step isolations, thereby improving safety and productivity.

COMPANY AFFILIATIONS

Malcar Corporation, St. Louis, MO   2007–Present
Scientific Systems, Louisville, KY   1995–2007
Johnson Chemicals, Boston, MA   1993–1995

Prior to 1993, held a variety of positions in chemical process development in Denmark, England, and France.

EDUCATION

Washington University, St. Louis, MO   M.B.A. 2006
University of Kentucky, Louisville, KY   M.A. Chemistry 1988
University of Massachusetts, Amherst, MA   B.A. Chemistry 1986

PATENTS

U.S. Patent 0,000,000–Process for polymerization of vinyl pyridine
U.S. Patent 0,000,000–Preparation of polymerizable monoeric esters

REFERENCES

Available on request

Jose Diaz

4322 Dadeland Road
Miami, FL 33333
Home: (506) 555-6787
Cell: (506) 555-7234
Jose_Diaz@xxx.com

Objective

Chief financial officer or senior administrative officer for a midsized company or controller for a larger organization.

Background Summary

More than 35 years of diversified financial and administrative experience with specific involvement and accomplishments in the areas of:

Accounting Management   Financial Reporting

Budgeting and Cost Controls   Human Resources

Information Systems Design   Management Information Systems

Manufacturing/Operations/Sales   Inventory and Distribution Management

Professional Experience

Carson's Baking Company, Miami, Florida (1987–Present)

Vice President, Finance and Administration (1993–Present)

Assistant Vice President/Controller (1989–1993)

Controller (1987–1989)

Responsible for all financial and administrative functions including cash flow projections, costing, insurance/risk management, banking relationships, contracts and legal documents, benefit plan compliance, and profitability improvements. Directed operational department functions when staffing and company needs dictated.

Professional Experience (continued)

Accomplishments include:

- Reduced both long-term debt and interest rate (from prime plus 2 to prime) while creating new, more flexible lines of credit.

- Controlled and reduced the accounts receivable days outstanding by improving the reporting of data and using it effectively to manage and speed collections through lockbox deposits.

- Managed the company's purchasing department contribution to profit by establishing criteria and plans that reduced costs of raw materials with results of $500,000 annual savings.

- Revised downward profit trends in sales and marketing by identifying savings in excess of $1,000,000. Eliminated wasteful programs through use of financial controls on selected expenses.

Lymon Farms Inc., Hallendale, Florida (1981–1987)

Controller

Directed and implemented the installation of an automated EDP system. Identified system needs; selected the hardware; and designed the software, reports, and controls to support the company's growth from $9 to $36 million.

Price Waterhouse, New York City, Denver, Miami (1974–1981)

Senior Auditor

Planned audit assignments and determined the scope of work to be performed. Prepared evaluations and suggestions for company management on improvements to internal accounting controls, tax strategies, and general management methods and procedures.

Education

Bob Jones University
Greenville, SC
B.S. Accounting, 1974

References available upon request.

Jacob Christy

76 Bradley Drive
Albert, NH 87443
(803) 555-8766
jacobchristy@xxx.com

Career Summary

I am a manufacturing executive experienced in biochemical, organic synthesis, sterile, and other manufacturing processes in highly regulated industries. For the last ten years, I have acted as a change agent involved in cost reduction programs, business resources, organizational restructuring, process improvement, and quality service enhancement. My strengths include new product introduction, business team direction, and integrating business systems. I am currently involved in implementing the Food Science Group's new strategic direction.

Laxmer Industries
Food Science Group
Vice President of Manufacturing (since 1992)
Transferred to the division's headquarters to take charge of all manufacturing, including 2,500 employees and three U.S. and two international plants. Currently hold line responsibility for the Food Science Group's manufacturing and support functions and for the supply of bulk products to Laxmer's other divisions. Annual production budget: $300–$500 million supporting up to $800 million in sales.

Key achievements include:
- Wide-ranging cost-improvement efforts have yielded cumulative cost reductions of $110 million per year, including annual labor cost reductions generating $35 million in savings.
- Reduced the management structure from seven layers to three. Implemented 70 self-managing work teams. Consolidated 16 production departments into seven and closed three of the original five manufacturing facilities.
- Completed capital investments totaling $370 million. This included the successful 2000 start-up of a state-of-the-art biotech plant in Indiana. Ongoing projects will bring capital investment to $580 million by 2010.
- Implemented increasingly complex regulatory obligations to agency satisfaction and reduced discharges to the environment by 47 percent. OSHA incident rate reduced by 64 percent over the past ten years.

Overall Results

Changed a conservative culture into a dynamic manufacturing organization composed of self-managing work teams supported by state-of-the-art technology and information systems. Final steps to create a paperless global manufacturing network are currently being implemented.

References Available

MANTOSE SEGWAI

235 Zephyr Court • Baltimore, MD 34332 • Cell: 619-555-9771

SUMMARY

Successful professional record in commercial real estate encompassing strategic marketing and business planning. Demonstrated ability to manage simultaneous projects and meet deadlines. Strong organizational and problem-solving ability.

PROFESSIONAL EXPERIENCE

Independent Real Estate Broker, February 2000–Present
- Primary focus is on the marketing, leasing, and selling of commercial real estate properties in the Baltimore metropolitan area. Responsible for generating sales contracts, negotiating leases, and developing strategic marketing plans for several retail and office developers.
- Initiated and negotiated key leases for clients in the warehousing and food distribution industries.

Director of Marketing, Barter & Associates, November 1990–February 2000
- Responsible for developing leasing and marketing plans to optimize market visibility and maximize occupancy levels.
- Directed marketing plans for Solony Square, a 700,000–square-foot multiuse complex, which resulted in an average 85 percent occupancy rate.

Vice President of Real Estate, J. De Moor Limited, April 1985–November 1990
- Responsible for all leasing, property management, and new real estate development for this leading real estate company.
- Performed new business feasibility studies and negotiated several major landlord-tenant contracts.
- Initiated the establishment of property sales and new business development divisions. Developed marketing plans designed to attract new business. Directed company's diversification strategy into real estate brokerage and leasing.

Vice President, Premier Investment Property, October 1980–April 1985
- Initiated management policies designed to improve the efficiency of retail and office leasing activities. Developed marketing strategies and plans to optimize tenant mix.

EDUCATION

Master of Business Administration, University of South Africa, Port Elizabeth 1979
Bachelor of Commerce, Marketing, University of South Africa, Port Elizabeth 1975

REFERENCES AVAILABLE UPON REQUEST

MARCO ANTONIO

3 Lime Road
Lincoln, WI 34867
(607) 555-7654
M.Antonio@xxx.com

OBJECTIVE

To use my experience as a chief financial officer and experience in government contracting and oil-field services companies to obtain a position in international business operations.

PROFESSIONAL EXPERIENCE

Armond Systems, 1994 to Present:
Vice President: Controlled the company's financial operations. In 2006 the company had losses of $20,000,000 with projected losses of $27,000,000 in 2007. Prepared and implemented a plan to reduce the losses in 2007 and to break even in 2008. This was accomplished by consolidating and centralizing the finance and administration functions from locations throughout the U.S. into a new and lower-cost facility in Dallas. This produced savings of more than $10,000,000 per year.

Implemented a plan to consolidate the data processing and communications systems providing an additional savings of $3,000,000 annually. Established a professional credit and collections organization that improved cash flow by $25,000,000 annually and reduced DSO from 79 days to 65 days in only 12 months. Provided guidelines for consolidating multiple logistics functions, creating a savings of $3,500,000 per year. Eliminated several product lines yielding an annual savings of $3,000,000.

Earlier, as controller of the third-largest division, successfully directed a geographically dispersed staff of 90 professional and clerical personnel in the areas of information systems, tax, treasury, financial reporting, financial analysis, purchasing, and equipment management. Provided guidance to managers in 80 locations throughout North America. This included research and engineering facilities, manufacturing operations, and other locations providing services directly to the client.

EDUCATION

B.S. and B.A. DePaul University, Chicago, IL

REFERENCES AVAILABLE

Gregg B. Gesse

1222 Clairborn Street • Oxnard, CA 67888

806-555-3386 • G.Gesse@xxx.com

Objective
A position utilizing my extensive background in finance and accounting.

Experience
1998–Present, Gesse Consulting Service
As an independent consultant, provide financial and accounting services to a wide range of clients. Specific expertise in the areas of tax, due diligence, and forensic accounting.

1990–1998, Bombay Cola Incorporated
Corporate Controller: Managed a staff of seven responsible for accounts payable, receivable, booking, and general ledger. Served as the corporation's primary resource on due diligence work in association with divestitures and acquisitions. Senior Accountant: Responsible for the development of an automated check-clearing process that reduced accounting turnaround time by 75 percent. Supervised three clerical workers who were responsible for bank reconciliation and credit.

1986–1990, Observatory Systems
Accountant: Assisted in the development of a five-year financial and accounting plan. Responsible for debits, credits, and various financial statements. Assumed the responsibilities of the accounting supervisor in her absence. Promoted from junior accountant after six-month probationary period.

1981–1986, Schwartz, Jacobs, and Irwin, CPAs
Staff Accountant: Recruited after college to enter the firm's training program. Consistently received "outstanding" evaluations.

1975–1981, Acme Distributing
Accounting Clerk: Assisted in financing my undergraduate education by working 30 hours per week in the accounts payable department.

References available on request.

Sunil Figuri

2122 Palegreen Drive
Stone Mountain, Georgia 30087
(404) 555-9295
Sunil.Figuri@xxx.com

Summary

More than 30 years of managerial leadership experience in providing practical and novel approaches to solving complex problems

Extensive and strong skills in:
- Sales, purchasing, and customer service
- Inventory control and physical distribution
- Government contracting

Experience

1990–Present
Jackson Equipment Company, Stillwell, GA
Assistant General Manager/Purchasing Manager
- Provided leadership and direction in building the company's growth from $250,000 to more than $5,000,000 in sales
- Directed the activities of a 42-member workforce, including office, warehousing, and customer service personnel
- Analyzed and initiated a computer system program designed to increase the efficiency of the customer service, order entry, purchasing, and inventory control departments
- Responsible for the development and implementation of all federal, state, and local government agency bids

Experience (continued)
- Directed all business activities for a $500,000 inventory, automated purchasing system
- Assumed overall general management responsibilities in the absence of the general manager

1978–1990
Dicky Floor Machine Company
Southeastern Sales Representative
- Handled all aspects of the sales process
- Provided personalized customer service
- Received "Top Sales Award" four times

Education
B.A., Georgia Institute of Technology, 1974
Atlanta, GA

References
Available on request

Jim Ditka   25 Second Street • Half Moon, Florida 44563

765-555-0987 • jimditka@xxx.com

Objective: Continuing my career in engineering with a special interest in automated systems and hardware design.

Education: University of Central Florida

Bachelor of Science in Engineering, 1990

Indian River Community College

Associate of Arts, Pre-Engineering

Honors: Phi Beta Lambda, March 1989

Experience: 1999–Present

Indian River Associates

Consultant

- Responsible for multiple client engagements and the overall quality of work performed.
- Play a pivotal role in the development of all training materials and curriculum.
- Specific expertise on jet engine combustion chambers.
- Instrumental in the development of clients in the defense, telecommunications, and maintenance industries.

1990–1999

Palmetto Engineering

Engineer

- Designed digital system programs for clients in the chemical and construction industries.
- Developed engineering applications for automated systems used extensively by the military.

References: Available upon request.

FRED RUSTLE • 22 Stonybrook Lane • Sheetrock, MO 63101
fredrustle@xxx.com • 788-555-5744

OBJECTIVE

A position in which I can utilize my thirty-plus years of experience in library science and archives work.

EXPERIENCE

United States Historical Society
Chief Archivist, 1996 to Present
• Responsible for the accurate analysis of manuscripts and related library materials for their historical and cultural significance.
• Developed a computerized library filing system to track work in progress and better control costs.

Washington University, St. Louis, MO
Archivist, 1980 to 1996
• Responsible for the preservation of Washington University's collection of pre-Corinthian art objects.
• Served as a historical reference resource for Dr. David Fouler's book *Reclaiming the World's Past*.
• Twice awarded the Martin J. Dewy Award for excellence in restoration.

Sotheby's International, New York, NY
Collection Estimator, 1975 to 1980
• Began career as a collection estimator and was subsequently promoted to a position of responsibility for the entire twelfth-century Chinese collection.

EDUCATION

New York University, New York, NY
B.A., Classics, 1975

SPECIAL SKILLS

• Fluent in German and Italian
• Familiar with all current library computer programs and databases

References available upon request

REBECCA BLOOM

23 Highwood Drive
Naperville, IL 60845
(708) 555-1693
Becky.Bloom@xxx.com

OBJECTIVE

A challenging position in product management, market research, or marketing communications.

QUALIFICATIONS

Extensive experience in conducting in-house and field research on commercial market and product opportunities for defense-based R&D division. Directed a product marketing department and have in-depth experience as senior product manager for telecommunications and related systems products. Additional experience as a regional sales manager, branch sales manager, and branch financial manager.

1998 to Present: Bloom Marketing Consulting
Currently provide marketing consulting services to a variety of client companies.

1990 to 1998: Sales and Marketing Manager, Alcan Inc.
Responsible for the marketing and sales of this company's line of telecommunications products. Designed and implemented the in-house and field marketing research to determine the possibility of successfully commercializing technology that resulted from defense department R&D projects.

1985 to 1990: Director of Marketing, Pampax Corp.
Directed overall marketing activities for this manufacturer of coatings, sealants, and related chemical products. Implemented activities including advertising, public relations, and trade shows to increase awareness of the company's products to prospective buyers. Nationally introduced a new polymer sealant product used extensively by the shipping industry.

1975 to 1985: Product Manager, Acme Chemicals
Developed the company's first marketing plan to explore new product introductions and expand the field sales force. Promoted to product manager after serving in the accounting and finance departments and in field sales.

1970 to 1975: Ensign, United States Navy

REFERENCES

Available on request.

ELLEN JONES

2345 Brandywood Court • Chisholm, NJ 98765 • 765-555-6547

ellenjones@xxx.com

OBJECTIVE

A position with a critical care or long-term health maintenance organization using my nursing experience.

EXPERIENCE

Nurses House Call Inc. • Senior Health Care Administrator, 2004 to Present
- Upgraded facility staffing through innovative RN and LPN recruiting efforts.
- Developed a home health-care program utilizing hospital aides, substantially reducing costs.
- Implemented a private duty health-care system resulting in savings of $320,000 annually.
- Investigated the feasibility of initiating a retirement community service. Recommendations are currently under evaluation by the board of directors.
- Provided unique infant-care services for employees of Clafo Manufacturing.
- Wrote an RN supervisors training program that was later adopted by the state health-care training service.

TLC Nursing Services • Administrative Manager, 1995 to 2004
- Designed and developed a plan that resulted in successful JCAHO accreditation.
- Simplified procedures for free initial consultation sessions.
- Established a 24-hour private duty hotline number and support service.
- Negotiated reduced fees for oxygen and medical equipment.
- Obtained Medicare/Medicaid certification.
- Streamlined operating procedures for administration of the nurse's aides contract service.

St. Judes of Northside • Supervising RN, 1990 to 1995
- Supervised a staff of 25, responsible for 24-hour health care services. Promoted to this position following a consistent level of excellent performance as a critical-care RN.
- Scheduled all RNs, LPNs, and nurses aides. Increased morale through implementation of a bidding process for shift assignments.
- Trained support personnel on effective hospital health-care techniques.

EDUCATION

B.S., Nursing, Stillwater College, Stillwater, OK

REFERENCES AVAILABLE

Elena Engles

23 Ryser Lane • Houston, Texas 66765

Home: 345-555-6789 • Cell: 345-555-6654 • elenaengles@xxx.com

Experience

Active Moving & Storage
1972–Present
Executive Assistant

- Upgraded credit and collection procedures by increasing communications with field marketing staff.
- Tabulated year-end closing results on time and under budget.
- Simplified the forecasting operations through the introduction of computerized planning software.
- Translated our French subsidiaries operation manual for use in the United States.
- Tested new administrative systems for potential introduction company-wide.
- Recommended an increase in support staff, which was adopted by senior management. Played a pivotal role in the recruiting and training of new staff.
- Participated in a quality improvement team, which identified several initiatives to increase worker morale and company profitability.
- Wrote a secretarial procedures manual on how to utilize the new computer system.
- Recorded all minutes for the annual Board of Directors meetings.

Education and Training

Harris Junior College
Associate's Degree in Administration

Ingram High School
Honors Graduate

Completed numerous self-study and classroom programs on a variety of administrative practices.

References

Available on request.

Donna Redmoon
170 High Street • Deerfield, IL 60015
(847) 555-2095 • Donna.Redmoon@xxx.com

Employment Objective
Seeking a challenging career position in the communications industry.

Education
1984–1986
DeVry Institute of Technology
Specialization in Communications and Management
Grade Point Average: 3.7/4.0

Work Experience
1992–present
Communications Analyst
Illinois University
Provide advice and counsel on communications issues impacting the university and its health care subsidiaries. Write press releases and interoffice memos as necessary. Review website for consistent messaging.

1986–1992
Assistant to the Vice President of Marketing
Humble Oil Company
Developed communications materials to assist in the business development process. Drafted speeches and proposals for the president of the company. Responsible for training summer interns and delegating duties.

1982–1986
Administrative Assistant
Chicago Journal
Provided administrative support to editors in the business and sports bureaus. Handled office procurement and office supply budget. Assisted with special events. Responsible for office equipment and maintenance.

References
Available upon request.

Dennis Faulkner

6191 Forest Hill Drive   Cell: 617-555-8877

Norcross, MA 01773   Email: faulkner@xxx.com

Experience

B.T. Realty & Management Services, Boston, MA, 2003 to Present

Vice President

- Senior management responsibility for real estate brokerage, complete property management services, and consulting. Specific focus is on providing strategic direction and perspective on operational issues and setting long-range strategies for the acquisition, lease, or sale of assets.

- Developed and implemented plans focused on achieving total customer satisfaction. This was achieved by meeting or exceeding performance projections and increasing occupancy rates, which led to consistent levels of profitability.

Davco, Inc., Nashville, TN, 1995 to 2003

Vice President—Development

- Overall responsibility for restaurant development including real estate construction, design, property management, franchise development, and contract administration. Scope of responsibility included direction over Slurpee franchise subsidiaries in St. Louis; Washington, D.C.; Baltimore; and the eastern shore of Maryland.

- Reported to the president and directed the activities of a professional staff of nine people, an administrative budget of $500,000, and a capital budget of $10 million.

- Successfully completed market analysis and site penetration correlations for 25 metropolitan markets. Developed 54 company-owned restaurants and consulted in the development of 130 franchise restaurants.

Bubba Hut, Inc., Austin, TX, 1984 to 1995

Senior Director of Property Management

- Oversaw an administrative budget of $1 million and a capital budget of $28 million for new units and $24 million for remodels. National responsibility for new property development, management of existing properties, and contract administration. Served as corporate liaison to the franchise community on all property management issues.

Experience (continued)

- Directed the activities of a corporate and a five-division property management staff.

- Served as a member of the corporate management team directly responsible for strategic planning and departmental budgeting.

- Successfully developed and implemented a site demographic and sales projection model for two restaurant markets.

- Member of a corporate management team that successfully oversaw the remodeling of the entire system of company-owned Bubba Hut restaurants.

Divisional Director of Property Management

- Initially responsible for the development of new properties and the management of existing properties in the Southern division. Responsibilities were expanded to include the Western division and a total of 22 states. Directed the activities of a 20-person staff consisting of real estate, construction, and support personnel with an administrative budget of $750,000 and a capital budget of $38 million.

- Member of Divisional Management team that supervised all field support groups for 450 company-owned Bubba Hut Restaurants.

Real Estate and Construction Manager

- Individually managed the acquisition and construction of restaurants in three states.

- Averaged opening ten restaurants per year.

Education

Union College, Lincoln, NE
B.S. Business Administration

References

Provided on request.

Deborah Ingard

98 Mills Rd. • Hackenstown, NJ 89765 • (304) 555-7865 • ingard@xxx.com

Objective

A position that would utilize my extensive experience in sales and marketing.

Experience

Ingard Consulting Services, 2005–Present
Owner/manager of a company that provides consulting services on utility expenses for commercial and industrial accounts and for homeowners with adjustable rate loans. Determine if clients have obtained optimum services and provide information to reduce their costs and expenses. Audit accounts for accuracy to ensure that they have not been overcharged through errors in calculating adjustments.

Active Sportswear, 1990–2005
Owner/operator of screen-printing business servicing commercial accounts. Developed new business and managed a staff consisting of an artist, three operators, and a sales representative. Successfully built the business from a start-up operation to annual revenues of $230,000.

Atlas Energy & Automation, 1981–1990
Manager of Market Development (1987–1990). Managed $150 million electrical apparatus division of this multibillion-dollar company. Reported to Director of Marketing. Identified product opportunities in new and existing markets and provided technical and field support to sales in pursuing these markets. Prepared product initiation proposals containing design/ratings specifications for developmental products in the division.

Product Manager (1982–1987). Developed pricing, pricing strategies, product line requirements, forecasting, and sales promotion programs. Coordinated technical product and training materials for distributors, contractors, and consultants.

Assistant Product Manager (1981). Identified product needs, wrote specifications, developed pricing, and introduced products that generated $2.5 million in sales.

Education

Marquette University, Milwaukee, WI
B.S. Electrical Engineering

Marquette University, Milwaukee, WI
Masters in Business Administration

References available on request

NADINE MERCIER

21 Jason Drive • Cleveland, OH 45066 • (513) 555-3695 • nadinemercier@xxx.com

OBJECTIVE

A position in general management or customer service in a nonmanufacturing organization where my extensive experience in improving profits and customer satisfaction can help the organization achieve its goals and objectives.

PROFESSIONAL EXPERIENCE

1990 to Present
BST SERVICE CENTERS
- Regional Manager for sales, service, and support activities for branches located in Cincinnati, Louisville, Dayton, and Springfield/Columbus. Manage a staff of 10, including four branch managers. Responsible for overall customer service and quality for the entire operation.
- Developed and executed a business plan to build a top-quality customer service organization. Played a key role in obtaining Borden, Reynolds & Reynolds, NCR, James River, and Humana as new clients.
- Restructured the service and support departments, which improved overall customer satisfaction levels from 55 percent to 89 percent over three years.

1972 to 1990
MANNIUM CONTAINER CORP.
- District Manager for this sales, service, and support organization. Responsible for overall day-to-day operations. Supervised a staff of up to 20 through three direct reports.
- Introduced a major cost-reduction program, which consolidated operations and established a highly competitive sales and customer service organization.
- Developed client relationships with accounts including Litton, Queen City Metro, and Good Samaritan Hospital.
- Prior to becoming District Manager, held positions with Mannium Container in advertising, account management, customer service, and inside sales.

EDUCATION

A.A. in Management
Lackland Community College, San Antonio, TX

REFERENCES

Available on request.

Margaret Whitlock

102 Campbell Street • Los Angeles, CA 90003
Cell: (310) 555-8700 • Home: (310) 555-6234
margaretwhitlock@xxx.com

Objective

A challenging opportunity in insurance that will utilize my extensive
experience in computing and administrative skills

Experience

Universal Life Insurance Inc., Los Angeles, CA
1976–Present
Executive Secretary
• Provide administrative and secretarial assistance to the Vice Presidents
  of Marketing and Finance.
• Reorganized company filing system to allow for greater access to
  information.
• Initiated the purchase of computer equipment to increase productivity.
• Awarded "Employee of the Month" on seven separate occasions.
• Plan and coordinate all receptions during the annual employee meeting.
• Serve as coordinator for the United Way campaign. Achieved record
  results in 1990.
• Type 100 words per minute. Highly proficient with most Microsoft word
  processing and spreadsheet programs.

Education

• Completed company programs on administrative organization, word
  processing, time management, and office management.
• Completed 12 hours of Business Administration classes at UCLA.
• Graduated with honors from New Trier High School.

References

Furnished upon request

Jake Brown
1843 Pine Street
New Rochelle, NY 87554
(212) 555-8721
jakebrown@xxx.com

Multifunctional professional manager with more than 32 years of marketing and business experience is adept at identifying market opportunities, developing marketing strategies, and providing product and field support to successfully pursue these markets.

Accustomed to managing multiple highly critical, complex projects simultaneously and bringing them to satisfactory conclusions. Possesses ability to prepare competitive studies, cost estimates, scope definitions, and specifications that relate products to customer needs. Track record of increasing market share through astute pricing and sharp market timing.

Major Strengths
- Market Identification/Development
- Marketing Strategies
- Pricing/Forecasting
- Product Management
- Communications Services
- Sales Support/Training

Possesses strong organizational skills and the ability to develop, motivate, and train people coupled with leadership talent and communication skills. Proficient in translating complex technical data into information that can be understood and utilized by sales personnel and customers. Self-starter and early contributor. Recognized for take-charge attitude and high standards of performance.

Employment

Brown Consulting, Owner	1992–Present
Jackson Equipment, VP Marketing	1981–1992
Outline Automation, Director of Sales	1976–1981

References available upon request

CAROL GANNETTI

2 Bedford Way • Lincoln, LA 44543 • (708) 555-6787 • carolgannetti@xxx.com

POSITION SOUGHT

A management opportunity that would benefit from my experience in the development and management of hotel/motel units.

WORK EXPERIENCE

The Lodge on Buford Stream, Assistant Executive Manager, 1992–Present

- Responsible for overall operation of this 250-room luxury resort hotel and convention center. Supervise a staff of 120 through a direct staff of 15.
- Mediated a labor dispute with the International Association of Restaurant Workers. A new contract was successfully negotiated, thus avoiding a potentially crippling strike.
- Conceived the original concept for the convention center, which was subsequently adopted by the owners. Convention sales and related activities now account for 34 percent of operating profits.
- Recruited a support staff to provide increased management attention to potential profit-center opportunities.
- Created a model display for the convention center, which helped in obtaining financing from local investors.

Suburban Lodge, Assistant Manager, 1986–1992

- Engineered the refurbishing of this 125-year-old family-oriented vacation destination.
- Centralized food-service purchasing operations to increase efficiencies and savings.
- Budgeted costs of expansion into room rate increases.

River Terraces, Food and Beverage Manager, 1981–1986

- Documented cost increases by major vendors, resulting in a successful renegotiating of existing contracts. Efforts saved the hotel 35 percent in operating revenues.
- Acquired a neighboring property that allowed for expansion of hotel amenities, including golf and tennis facilities.

EDUCATION & TRAINING

University of Louisiana, Monroe, LA
B.A. Hotel Management

Numerous additional courses in accounting, marketing, and operations management.

References available upon request.

Bruce Pickenstein

2 Allen Drive • Buffalo, New York 14202

(978) 555-9087 • Cell: (978) 555-9537 • bruce_pickenstein@xxx.com

Objective

Seeking a position in the telecommunications industry that would benefit from my extensive experience in marketing and general management.

Experience

Pagenet Telecommunications, 1975–Present

Region Manager, 1995–Present
- Responsible for all operations in the Northeastern region.
- Supervise a staff of 10, consisting of sales, operations, engineering, and administrative support personnel.
- Region consistently ranked number one in the nation.

   Significant Accomplishments:
   - Accelerated the diversification of the product line from office-based telecommunications systems to an "open" environment accessible from either the home or office.
   - Conducted an industry analysis that led to a significant reorganization and restructuring. Profits increased 34 percent as a result of the reorganization.
   - Communicated significant changes in the industry that were likely to affect company operations, thus reducing stress and potential turnover.
   - Completed the sale of the Bitwell subsidiary for a $230,000 profit over purchase price.

Marketing Manager, 1988–1995
- Developed the company's first comprehensive marketing plan, which was adopted by the board of directors.
- Headed a multidistrict task force to identify new marketing objectives and opportunities for growth.

Sales Representative, 1975–1988
- Joined the company (originally named Jackson & Johnson Manufacturing) after military service. Marketed the full range of company products to clients nationwide.
- Seven-time winner of the "Golden Eagle" award for exceeding company sales objectives.

Education

State University of New York, Buffalo
Associate's Degree in Business Administration

References available upon request.

JEFFREY ATLAS

2 Adidas Lane
Beaverton, OR 98734
(867) 555-4532
jatlas@xxx.com

EXPERIENCE

Schlumbarker, Inc., Salem, OR (1990–Present)
Chief Operating Officer (2007–Present): Direct a staff of 10 professional and clerical personnel for the technology unit of the petroleum services group with annual revenues of $250,000. Division provides high-technology services to customers involved in oil and gas exploration. Provide administrative support to two regional and five division managers controlling more than 60 domestic operations within the unit.

Manager, Internal Consulting (2001–2007): Handled all aspects of the firm's internal consulting operations and worked closely with various business segment general managers on special projects, including audits, systems enhancements, manufacturing operation reviews, and merger/divestiture analysis. Recruited, developed, and managed high-potential trainees.

Controller (1996–2001): Managed a staff of 30 in the financial and data processing departments. Exercised functional supervision over controllers in five subsidiaries throughout Europe and Asia. Installed a new business computer and hardware system that increased the visibility of the company's North American profitability.

Manager, Corporate Accounting (1990–1996): Transformed the accounting department from a corporate to a divisional structure. Directed a staff of 20 professional and clerical personnel in the areas of accounting, financial reporting, forecasting, and budgeting.

Education

Boston University	B.A., Political Science
University of Massachusetts–Boston	B.S., Business
University of Massachusetts–Boston	M.B.A.
University of Massachusetts–Boston	M.A., Divinity

Military

United States Navy, Chaplain Corps

References

Provided on request

LATOYA REYNOLDS

76 Stone Blvd. • Detroit, Michigan 45623
(313) 555-9822 • L.Reynolds@xxx.com

- Highly experienced manager in the areas of marketing, strategic planning, and new product development. Increased profits by 110 percent and brand market share from 25 percent to 31 percent for a mature $300 million business over seven years.
- Open to any size company.
- Delivered record profits in six out of the past seven years.
- Instituted new-product development process accounting for 26 percent of sales volume and six new line extensions.
- Proven ability in marketing management, marketing research, innovative business development, and strategic changes in corporate direction and organizational structure. Key player in mergers and acquisitions.
- Managed the development and installation of a major strategic change in a profitable $500 million business to further increase earnings by more than 90 percent within four years. Reduced costs by $25 million annually.
- Developed and launched $145 million new product line.

WORK EXPERIENCE

1997–Present: Lyndon Consumer Products, Director of Marketing (Earlier positions included Category Manager, Brand Manager, and Brand Assistant)

1990–1997: Amway Products, Director of Marketing Research

1986–1990: Orloff & Kreigg, Marketing Research Manager

1980–1986: Lamhoff Pharmaceuticals, District Sales Manager (Earlier positions included Territory Manager and District Sales Representative)

EDUCATION

University of Illinois–Chicago
B.A. Marketing and Management

Continuing education at Detroit's Wayne State University as needed. Classes have included such courses as PowerPoint Essentials for the Business World, Marketing 550, and Integrating your Products with Web Marketing.

REFERENCES

Provided on request.

BOBBIE HOLLOWAY

12 Broad St.
New York, NY 10433
(212) 555-6543
bholloway@xxx.com

EXPERIENCE

1978–present
Champion Products
Project Manager (1987–present)

- Consolidated regional centers, which saved more than $10 million per year while simultaneously improving service levels. Recipient of Champion "Citation for Success" Award.
- Introduced a new equipment-leasing program reducing overall costs by $2 million per year.
- Renegotiated the service contracts for the northeastern region providing efficiencies and increasing profitability by 5 percent.
- Brought accounting and DP operations from tenth place to first place among 12 offices in the company. Demonstrated a consistent ability to meet corporate quality and performance standards.
- Computerized a manual payroll system cutting overhead by 8.3 percent and improving employee morale.
- Consolidated the Johnston branch into the New York City operation while maintaining employee morale and productivity. Achieved savings of 22 percent over a three-year period of time.
- Renegotiated employee labor agreements based on a "flexible work" agreement. The new contract allowed for greater flexibility on the part of management to schedule work shifts while allowing union employees to increase earnings through an innovative management/employee incentive program. Based on the success of this program I was invited to address the National Association of Project Managers to review our implementation efforts.
- Began career with the company following graduation from high school. Started as a stockroom employee.

EDUCATION

University of New York, New York, NY
B.A. in Business

New York City Community College
A.A. in Business Administration

REFERENCES

Provided on request

Anne White

2 Tabor Rd. • Las Vegas, NV 99999 • 301-555-6146 • annewhite@xxx.com

Objective
A challenging position in the food service industry.

Experience
Barnes Food Service, Inc., Las Vegas, NV
1996–Present
Director of Food Service Operations

- Responsible for overall management of a staff of 50 individuals involved in all aspects of food preparation and delivery.
- Design the menus and food specials for seven local-area casino/hotel food service operations.
- Manage a food service budget of $1.2 million.

Le Cote De Mure, Miami, FL • 1986–1996
Executive Chef

- Managed a staff of eight assistant chefs and related food service professionals.
- Twice awarded four stars by the Luskin Guide for dining excellence.

Jimmy's by the Sea, Boston, MA • 1980–1986
Assistant Chef

- Served as chief apprentice to Chef Jean-Paul Rambeaux.
- Extensive training in seafood and pastry preparation.
- Assumed chief chef responsibilities in the absence of Chef Rambeaux.

Education
The Culinary Institute, Dallas, TX
Honors Graduate, 1979

University of Nevada, Las Vegas, NV
M.B.A., 2003

References available

Nahid Mahjoub

123 Oceanside Drive • Tettly, TN 22343 • 608-555-3245 • N_Mahjoub@xxx.com

Summary

Energetic and enthusiastic. Highly experienced at working with all types of individuals. Able to relate effectively and efficiently to students and senior-level managers. Recently retired following 35 years of service at South Carolina A&T.

Experience

South Carolina A&T, 1973–2008

Registrar, 1984–2008
• Responsible for the efficient registration of 3,500 students.
• Assisted in the conversion of the registration process from a manual approach to a computerized bid system.
• Increased levels of "customer" satisfaction based on annual student surveys of the registration process.
• Organized and implemented the annual freshman orientation to class registration. Conducted group and individual meetings on registration process and procedures. Wrote an instruction manual for inclusion in the freshman orientation handbook.
• Supervised a staff of 20, including part-time undergraduate and graduate students.

Administrative Assistant, 1973–1984
• Provided administrative support to the Dean of the College of Arts and Sciences. Assisted in the compilation and organization of his files for the book *Onward Old A&T*.
• Coordinated support staff for all receptions and conventions.
• Handled daily schedule and routine correspondence.
• Served as the department assistant for inter-fraternity functions and events.

Education

Mechlenberg High School, Honor Graduate

References

Available upon request.

SYLVIA ODENWOOD

3 Briscut Lane • Montrose, CA 93198

310-555-9876 • cell: 310-555-9095 • sylviaodenwood@xxx.com

SUMMARY OF PROFESSIONAL EXPERIENCE

A conscientious and hardworking individual, effective at creating an environment in which the love of learning can be developed. Eager to take my experience in public education and apply it to private industry. Consistently challenged to bring out the best in others.

OVERVIEW: Thirty-five years as a successful high school instructor of history and English at Oak Valley High School. Received the Dobbs County Award for Teaching Excellence on seven separate occasions. Recognized by the school board for introducing innovative teaching methods into the classroom. Effective at motivating hard-to-teach children. Author of the textbook *Fundamentals of English*, published by Roberts & Oral Publishing.

MANAGEMENT EXPERIENCE: Maintain a motivated classroom through the use of innovative teaching techniques. Chaired the school committee's subgroup on increasing parental involvement in the school system. Coordinator of the 2002 United Way fundraising effort, which achieved record results.

COMMUNICATION EXPERIENCE: Regular contributor to the *Oak Valley High School Gazette*. Highly effective at communicating with emotional and/or unmotivated students. Able to synthesize information into forms that are quickly understood by diverse segments of the population.

EFFECTIVENESS: Commended by the school board as a person who "truly makes a difference in others' lives." Strong ability to motivate subordinates, peers, and all members of the team.

ADMINISTRATIVE SKILLS: Highly organized with an acute attention to detail. Responsible for the reorganization of manual filing systems to computerized information retrieval systems. Process increased efficiency and users' ability to quickly access information.

EDUCATION

M.A. English, University of the West, Rosemead, CA

M.A. Education, University of the West, Rosemead, CA

B.A. English, University of the West, Rosemead, CA

REFERENCES

Available upon request.

JEAN SMILEY

8254 Argorn Court, Apartment 554

Eden Prairie, MN 22322

506-555-7876

jeansmiley@xxx.com

OBJECTIVE

An executive secretary position

EXPERIENCE

Cates, Miller & Irwin CPAs, 2001–Present
Position: *Executive Secretary*
Responsibilities: Schedule appointments, maintain files, expedite travel procedures, and handle routine correspondence. Promoted to this position based on receiving excellent reviews from two previous supervisors.

Oleo Manufacturing, 1996–2001
Position: *Marketing Secretary*
Responsibilities: Provided administrative support to the director of marketing and three members of his staff. Responsible for all administrative procedures. Assisted in implementing an IBM administrative software system to replace the existing manual system.

Homemaker, 1978–1996

Rockwell Imports, 1974–1978
Position: *Secretary*
Responsibilities: Promoted from the clerical pool to provide secretarial support to the vice president of sales. Consistently received excellent evaluations.

EDUCATION

Wausau Community College, Wausau, WI
Completed several courses in Secretarial and Administrative Studies.

References available upon request

IRWIN C. SAVAGE

123 Glendale Dr. • Mt. Auburn, MA 01111 • 617-555-6876
irwinsavage@xxx.com

OBJECTIVE

A position in international trade that would utilize my background in import/export and my knowledge of the French and German languages.

EXPERIENCE

1991 to Present: Auckland International Distributors   Senior Sales Agent

- Responsible for more than $2 million in new sales of French-made construction equipment to U.S.–based home manufacturers.
- Negotiated a free-trade agreement between 27 French building manufacturers.
- Coordinated the introduction of German-manufactured synthetic plywood products into the U.S. marketplace.
- Negotiated trans-Atlantic shipping rates as an alternative to airborne traffic, resulting in savings of $100,000.
- Recruited and hired an overseas sales staff of 10. Sales team consistently exceeded marketing objectives by 21 to 45 percent.
- Received the "Order of Excellence" award from the British Department of Economic Incentives in recognition of my work in fostering an environment of economic support between the United States and Great Britain.

1969 to 1991: United States Army

- Entered the service following graduation from West Point as a Second Lieutenant. Promoted through the ranks and retired honorably as a Lieutenant Colonel in 1991.
- Spent the majority of career in operations and shipping at key bases in Germany, France, and Asia.
- Supervised a staff of up to 250 enlisted personnel.

ADDITIONAL INFORMATION

Fluent (written and verbal) in French and German.
Limited knowledge of Mandarin.
Highly proficient in logistical and material-handling software programs.

EDUCATION

United States Army Academy, West Point, NY
B.A. Engineering 1969

REFERENCES

Available on request.

ROBERT STEEL

123 La Cienega • Sherman Oaks, CA 92113 • Bobby_Steel@xxx.com • 310-555-9977

SUMMARY

More than 20 years of experience with the Los Angeles Police Department and 10 years as a private investigator/security consultant with the nation's leading private security firm.

EXPERIENCE

<u>Jackson, Cooks & Balboli, Investigator, 2000 to Present</u>
• Provided investigative and security services to individuals and corporate clients.
• Designed emergency response system for Telecomp Corporation. Trained company security personnel in emergency systems.
• Successfully investigated a $350 million stock fraud swindle. Final report was subsequently given to the FBI and resulted in seven convictions.
• Provided personal security protection for numerous personalities and celebrities.

<u>Los Angeles Police Department, 1980 to 2000</u>
Sergeant, 1995 to 2000
• Managed and assigned duty shifts for 15 patrol officers.
• Provided counseling and career direction for officers seeking to transition from the department.
• Participated in community outreach programs at local high schools to discuss careers with the police department and answer questions about public safety.

Patrol Officer, 1980 to 1990
• Served as a foot patrol officer in the La Cienega/El Cajoun area of Los Angeles County.
• Strengthened community relations with the police department through outreach efforts and increased visibility.
• Awarded several citations for "Distinguished Service."

<u>United States Navy</u>
Ensign, Military Police, 1975 to 1980

EDUCATION

University of California–Los Angeles
B.A. Political Science

References available on request.

Reggie Phillips
23 Richmond Ave. • Miami, FL 34567
305-555-6785 • Cell: 305-555-9823
Reggie_Phillips@xxx.com

Summary
Extensive experience in retail store management and sales. Proven and demonstrated track record in increasing store profitability and turnarounds. Available for either long-term or contract consulting assignments.

Experience
Marshall Jones & Company, 1976–Present
Merchandising Manager, 1996–Present
- Responsible for purchasing children's toys for this 150-store southeastern retail chain.
- Increased profitability of the toy department by 35 percent annually for the past five years.
- Introduced the "Wally War Machine" to the southeastern market. This toy, directed at boys ages 10 to 15, was the most successful introduction in the past eight years.
- Introduced a new merchandising strategy that resulted in a decrease in returns and improved efficiencies in ordering.
- Supervised a staff of 10 consisting of junior buyers and support personnel.

Senior Buyer, 1986–1996
- Responsible for negotiating and purchasing sporting goods equipment for the flagship Miami store.
- Successfully negotiated the introduction of oversized tennis rackets into the Florida marketplace.
- Created an innovative packaging concept for baseball equipment, resulting in a 45 percent increase in sales.

Department Head, 1980–1986
- Responsible for sales in the men's furnishing department.
- Supervised a staff of nine full- and part-time sales representatives.

Sales Clerk, 1976–1980
- Responsible for personal sales in the men's furnishing department.
- Received the "President's Award" for excellence in service and personal selling.

Education
Miami Dade High School

References available upon request.

MILDRED DUTTA

122 Keystone Court • Torrance, CA 99876

310-555-7855 • Cell: 310-555-6439 • milly.dutta@xxx.com

SUMMARY

Began culinary career as a waitress in a small diner in the Midwest. Progressed through a series of positions until I purchased and renovated the Old Pie Inn in 1987. After several years, my partner and I started a catering business specializing in traditional American foods and desserts. The American Food Catering Corporation of Dallas, Texas, has recently purchased the business.

CAREER OBJECTIVE

Seeking a consulting position in the food service or hospitality industry.

QUALIFICATIONS

More than 30 years of experience in the management of a "Three Star" restaurant. Founder and former CEO of the West's largest and most profitable catering organization. Extensive management experience and knowledge of food purchasing and cash flow systems.

ACCOMPLISHMENTS

• Restored a 10-year-old unprofitable restaurant to profitability in less than 12 months.
• Developed a marketing plan for a food-service catering system, which achieved profitability in three months and generated more than $150,000 profit in its first year.
• Columnist for *American Cuisine* magazine. Author of more than 120 articles on food preparation and service.
• Serve as the regional representative for the California Food Institute. Elected to chair the business ethics roundtable by my peers.

EDUCATION

Completed one year of business studies at the University of California–Los Angeles. Learned accounting and bookkeeping skills through evening courses at the LaSalle Extension of the University of Southern California. Avid reader of business and restaurant trade publications and periodicals.

REFERENCES

Available upon request.

MICHAEL THOMAS

3208 Bridge Avenue • Allentown, PA 12342 • (308) 555-9834 • michaelthomas@xxx.com

OBJECTIVE

Executive position requiring strong financial, operational, and administrative skills.

SUMMARY

Senior executive experienced in general management, operational start-ups, real estate, and corporate finance. Specific skills in complex debt and equity transactions, acquisitions, and workouts. Hands-on accounting and budgetary experience. Strong interpersonal and presentation skills.

Charter Financial Corporation, 1993–Present • Executive Vice President and Chief Financial Officer

- The company owns and manages 20 long-term health facilities in 10 states.

- Responsibilities include capital formation; mergers and acquisitions; lender/investor relations; and design and implementation of accounting, budgeting, and reporting systems.

Recreation Capital Group, 1989–1993 • President and Chief Executive Officer

- Recruited to form, capitalize, and manage this privately owned merchant bank that financed hotel properties nationwide.

- Successfully raised $31 million equity venture capital from three public companies.

- Arranged a $75 million line of credit to finance operations.

- Responsible for the installation of all operating procedures, organizational structure, marketing, construction management, property valuation, and credit underwriting.

- Installed all accounting, MIS, benefits, and risk management systems.

Morgan Trust Company, 1970–1989 • Executive Vice President

- Promoted to this position in 1980, reporting directly to the President.

- Managed the real estate department of the nation's 17th largest bank.

- Managed a staff of 30 professionals responsible for a real estate portfolio of $3.2 billion.

- Increased the loan portfolio by $475 million.

- Formed a real-estate investment banking division, which successfully executed the first letter of credit backed by commercial paper on Wall Street.

EDUCATION

M.B.A., School of Business, University of California–Berkeley, 1970

B.A., Economics, University of California–Berkeley, 1968

REFERENCES

Available on request.

KISHA LEE
1 Elm Street • Newtown, AL 22321 • 310-555-9345 • Kisha.Lee@xxx.com

SUMMARY
Seeking a position in the travel industry. Have extensive experience as a travel agent and flight attendant.

EXPERIENCE
All-World Travel Agency, 2000 to Present
Senior Agent
- Assist travelers in developing vacation and business travel plans. Use expertise developed in personal knowledge of many locations in advising clients.
- Increased vacation clients from an initial base of 25 to 195. Over 70 percent of clients are repeat customers.
- Developed 13 corporate clients as customers. Impressed corporate clients with knowledge of destination cities and appreciation for maximizing budget dollars.
- Created a marketing plan for All-World Travel that was adopted by the home office.
- Won trips to Cyprus, Rome, and the Virgin Islands.

Trans-World Airlines, 1991 to 2000
Flight Attendant
- Provided customer service and flight safety services to passengers on domestic and international routes.
- Awarded President's Commendation for excellence in service.

Fort Dix School System, 1987 to 1991
Teacher
- Taught general education courses to students in the fourth through seventh grades.

EDUCATION
Jefferson College, Hillsboro, MO
B.A. Education

Martin Community College, Martin, MO
A.A. Secretarial Sciences

REFERENCES
Available on request.

Mack Ford

3 Florissant Rd. • St. Louis, MO 63221 • 314-555-7654 • mackford@xxx.com

Objective

A position utilizing my extensive experience in automotive repair and service station management.

Summary

More than 30 years' experience managing service stations and providing customer automotive service.

Experience

Cullen Service Station, St. Louis, MO
Manager, 1975–Present

- Responsible for customer service, management of staff, and daily record keeping. Provide personal service to clients with complex automotive mechanical issues.
- Conduct automotive seminars at Florissant Valley Community College for individuals interested in learning more about automotive repair.
- Implemented a training program for Cullen Service Station employees to increase customer levels of satisfaction. Efforts were rewarded by an increase in repeat customer traffic.
- Reduced turnover among service staff by 55 percent by implementing a performance-based compensation system, including base salary and bonuses.

Jackson Automotive, St. Louis, MO
Sales Agent, 1971–1975

- Sold Ford automotive products to clients in the St. Louis area. More than 60 percent of sales came from repeat, satisfied customers.
- Initiated a sales training/customer service training program for all new sales employees.

Education

University of Missouri–St. Louis
A.A. Business

References

Provided on request.

Lemar Johnston

1221 Johnson Ferry
Capital Grove, MD 34332
406-555-7899
Lemar_Johnston@xxx.com

OBJECTIVE

A senior scientist position that would utilize my education and
extensive experience in analyzing synthetic gases.

EDUCATION

University of New York, New York, NY
Ph.D. Chemical Engineering, 1975

University of New York, New York, NY
M.S. Chemistry, 1972

Amherst College, Amherst, MA
B.S. Chemistry, 1970

EXPERIENCE

Duquant Chemical Company, Senior Analyst
1980 to Present
• Conduct complex chemical analysis in support of the oil and gas
  industry. Supervise a staff of three analysts and interns.
• Prepare reports for senior management on the viability of utilizing
  hydrogen as a method for the removal of liquefied gas from shale
  rock.

EXPERIENCE (continued)

• Expertise in most PC-based systems used for the analysis of gas properties. Designed an innovative software program to assist in the analysis of gases and other chemicals.

Adams Research Institute, Senior Scientist
1970 to 1980

• Analyzed chemical compounds to determine toxicity levels. Project was a joint venture funded by the EPA and Dulles Chemical Company.
• Testified before a Senate subcommittee on the potential adverse aspects of recycling certain automotive byproducts.
• Awarded an "Adams Scholars" bonus for contributions to the field of chemical analysis.

REFERENCES AVAILABLE

Eric Sparling

1223 Middle Court Pass

St. Louis, MO 63133

314-555-6709

Cell: 314-555-8433

Eric.Sparling@xxx.com

Summary

Highly experienced and accomplished attorney. Primary emphasis on real estate and construction. Extensive litigation and corporate experience.

Partner, 1986–Present

Ward, Mondell & Cleaver

- Responsible for the development of the firm's first construction practice area. Expanded the business from start-up to more than $400,000 in billings. Recruited lateral partners from other Midwest law firms to assist in the expansion. Elevated to partnership in 1995.

- Coordinate all of the firm's law school recruiting activities. Chaired select task force on recruitment strategies and focus. Identified key schools and initiated comprehensive recruitment strategy. Results: increased hiring by 35 percent and lowered costs by 12 percent.

- Served as lead counsel on *Whitey vs. June*, which established precedents for construction injury claims in the Seventh District Court. Case featured in *American Lawyer Journal* and on CBS News.

Summary (continued)

• Argued *Beetle vs. Framingham Board of Sewers*, resulting in a $2.5 million award for the defendant. Court decision upheld on appeal before the state supreme court. Successfully argued position before Judge Edward Haskell.

• Three-time recipient of the Beaverton Award for legal support of the construction industry.

Lt. J.G.; Legal Affairs Department, 1978–1986
U.S. Navy

Education
Vanderbilt University, Nashville, TN
J.D. 1978

Washington University, St. Louis, MO
B.A. History 1975

References available upon request.

Ernest Angelee

7 Baptist Rd
Tulsa, OK 99876
908-555-6666
ernestangelee@xxx.com

Objective

To use my extensive experience and knowledge of book
publishing with a company committed to teamwork and consensus
decision-making.

Professional Experience

1995 to Present, Roberts & Oral Publishing, Managing Editor
Responsible for the editorial quality for the "Good News Today"
series of books. Increased the number of inspirational books from
10 to 50. Manage a staff of 14, consisting of junior editors, copy-
writers, clerical staff, and contract authors. Editor for the bestseller
Louisville Tithing by William Graham.

1989 to 1995, Sunlight Books, Assistant Managing Editor
Responsible for overseeing contract authors, clerical staff, and two
junior editors. Edited *Confucians' Revenge*, winner of the Leo and
Peavey awards. Successfully recruited noted author Harry Longbau
from Sundance Publishing to collaborate with Robert Cassidy on
their bestselling novel *Just a Couple of Guys*.

Professional Experience (continued)

1988 to 1989, Freelance Author
Completed the novel *Gypsy Moth* and produced freelance articles that appeared in *Ladies' Home Journal* and *Esquire*. Collaborated with Bill Shakesworth on the off-Broadway production of *Running Down Center Avenue*. Play won the Jose Foote Award for best new drama of 1989.

1986 to 1988, *Wichita Eagle-Beacon*, Features Editor
Managed a staff of five responsible for producing the weekly and weekend features section. Introduced columns by Larry Owens and Betsy Hoagland. Recognized by senior management for revamping the food section to include graphics and increased quality of writing.

1984 to 1986, *Johnstown Tribune*, Features Writer
Produced weekly columns on food and home decorating. Created the paper's first society column under the name "Rudolph on the Town."

1981 to 1984, *Boston Globe*, Administrative Assistant
Provided assistance to the features, business, and sports departments.

Education

B.A., English, Boston University

References available.

CARL WEATHERLY · 1 Meadow Lane • Arlington, VA 55676

Home: 809-555-9833 • Cell: 809-555-9665 • carlweatherly@xxx.com

OBJECTIVE

A position utilizing my background in military law and more than 30 years of service in the United States Army. Currently plan to retire from active duty at the conclusion of this year. Retiring with the rank of major.

SUMMARY

Extensive experience in research, litigation, and negotiations involving complex legal issues. Ability to relate equally effectively to enlisted personnel, senior-level officers, and high-ranking civilian personnel. Adept at the management of the military legal system and its interactions with the civilian bar.

EDUCATION

George Washington University, Ashburn, VA • J.D., cum laude

Army Intelligence Institute, Arlington, VA • B.A. Military Science

Emphasis on Logistics and Command

EXPERIENCE

United States Army

Chief Liaison, 1994 to Present

Coordinate all legal activities for the 195th Joint Infantry. In addition to day-to-day legal operations, responsible for the dissemination of information from various Senate and House committees to senior command officers in the joint forces. Coordinate preparation of all ongoing litigation and plea bargaining. Supervise a staff of 27.

Chief of Staff, 1986 to 1994

Provided tactical and technical legal information and feedback to the Commanding Officer, 7th Battalion–Korea. Personally conducted all significant trial work. Managed a staff of 15.

Executive Officer, 1981 to 1986

Served in the number-two legal position to the chief attorney of Fort Johnston. Supervised a staff of 12 attorneys and paralegals. Responsible for all daily legal activity. Awarded Army citation for excellence.

Infantry Officer, 1975 to 1981

Commanded units of up to 400 troops in the United States and overseas. Twice awarded commendations for excellence in command.

REFERENCES AVAILABLE UPON REQUEST

Billy Joe Tolliver
23 Cranberry Drive
Fort Smith, Arkansas 33445
(718) 555-7644 • B.Tolliver@xxx.com

BACKGROUND SUMMARY

• Highly experienced coach.
• Experienced in professional sports, military, and educational institutions.
• Excellent communication and interpersonal skills.

PROFESSIONAL EXPERIENCE

1995–Present
Dekalb County School System, Educator and Coach
Teach world history to students in the 9th–12th grades.
• Effective at motivating students to achieve excellence.
• Twice awarded the Cybrus Award for teaching excellence.
• Counsel students seeking alternative educational direction. Maintain comprehensive and current knowledge of local-area vocational and technical schools. Dramatically impacted the percentage of students going on for advanced training.
• Head coach for men's football and baseball. Football teams have consistently achieved winning seasons. Division runner-up in 1996, 1997, and 2003. Baseball team ranked number 12 in the nation. Four former students currently playing in the professional leagues.

1985–1995
 U.S. Marine Corps, Master Sergeant
• Entered the corps as a private and was promoted through the ranks.
• Served in the military police at bases in Germany, Korea, and the Philippines.
• Coached inter-military football team to division championship. Honorably discharged.

1981–1983
 Detroit Lions Professional Football, Defensive Lineman

EDUCATION

B.A., History, 1985
University of Arkansas, Fayetteville, AK

References available upon request.

BARRY ROBERT JONES

123 Barney Avenue • Dallas, Texas 54322

Home: 607-555-6677 • Cell: 607-555-7322 • Email: B.Jones@xxx.com

OBJECTIVE

A position utilizing my background and experience in marketing and sales.

EDUCATION:

George Williams University, Memphis, TN
M.B.A., 2008

University of Memphis
Bachelor of Business Degree in 1991
Varsity Football and Baseball

EXPERIENCE

Empire Insurance Company
Agent, 2001 to Present
• Responsible for the development of clients in the tri-city area.
• Consistently met or exceeded sales goals.
• Winner of the "Golden Circle" award for sales excellence.

Allmar Insurance
Sales Representative, 1994 to 2001
• Marketed a variety of business forms and supplies to manufacturing firms in the southeast.
• Established the company's presence in the Nashville market.
• Introduced 10 new products in the six-state territory.
• Consistently met or exceeded sales objectives.

Hillman Fastening Systems
Sales Representative, 1991 to 1994
• Sold the Hillman line of fastening systems to customers.
• Handled 20 key accounts with responsibility for selling the full line of products on the construction site.
• Twice awarded the "President's Club" award.

References available upon request.

Chapter 6

Sample Cover Letters

This chapter contains sample cover letters for people pursuing a wide variety of jobs and careers.

There are many different styles of cover letters in terms of layout, level of formality, and presentation of information. These samples also represent people with varying amounts of education and work experience. Choose one cover letter or borrow elements from several different cover letters to help you construct your own.

Jim Brinkman
4 Lion Drive
Lincoln, MA 01774

January 6, 20__

Alan Jones
ABCD, Incorporated
34 Terry Road
Lincoln, MA 01773

Dear Mr. Jones:

During a meeting last week, Neal Bortz discussed your company's history
and recent growth and suggested I write to you. While he was not sure that
you had an immediate need for someone like me, he did feel that we might
have a mutual interest in getting together for a brief meeting.

To give you a better idea of what I bring to the table, I've enclosed a copy of
my resume, which lists my experience and potential contributions.

I would welcome a brief meeting with you to discuss what specific
contributions I could make to your organization. I'll call you on Monday to
see when such a meeting might be set up.

Sincerely,

Jim Brinkman

JANE ALEXANDER

3 Roe Street • Cleveland, OH 67554 • (216) 555-6712 • J.Alexander@xxx.com

March 14, 20__

Mike Jennings
Action Insurance
45 Rand Road
Cleveland, OH 66546

Dear Mr. Jennings:

Your company is well-known throughout the insurance industry. I've also been aware of your advertisements in various publications over the years. As the enclosed resume outlines, I have had more than thirty years of progressive responsibility in the insurance industry.

Recently, I reviewed Empire Insurance's entire divisional operation and implemented initiatives that reduced expenses by more than $400,000. This was done without any interruption to client service. I feel that I could also positively contribute to the bottom line of Action Insurance by bringing my skills and years of experience to your company.

I would like the opportunity to personally discuss any positions you may currently have open that would be a good match with my background. I'll call you next week to arrange a time to meet.

Sincerely,

Jane Alexander

Yonin Frank

5169 West 22nd Street
Appleton, WI 54911

August 5, 20__

Jim Karns
Lakely Products
445 Green Street
Green Bay, WI 54303

Dear Mr. Karns:

I read with interest your recent advertisement for a Personnel Manager.
My background closely matches the requirements in the advertisement.
Some of my recent accomplishments include:
* Designed a nonexempt salary schedule from local survey data and admin-
  istered the exempt salary plan within company policy and budgetary
  guidelines.
* Managed and published a manpower planning report to HR and Finance
  for actual budget and forecasting head count.
* Managed and distributed payment for the senior management incentive
  bonus program.
* Provided statistical data toward the preparation of AAP.

My background has enabled me to be very successful in a fast-paced
growth environment. I have enclosed my resume for your review, and I
look forward to meeting you in person to discuss how my talents can lead
to superior results for you. Please feel free to call or email me to set up a
meeting.

Sincerely,

Yonin Frank
(920) 555-2774
y.frank@xxx.com

September 4, 20__

Ad #345
Boston Globe
Boston, MA 09877

To Whom It May Concern:

My experience and talents match closely your requirements for a Director of Marketing.

YOUR REQUIREMENTS	MY EXPERIENCE
Innovative Person	I have created new marketing niches by differentiating my products from those traditionally used.
Strategic Leadership	I have headed the strategic and business marketing planning for the largest division of Plogue Industries.
Strong Technical Skills	My skills are backed up by both academic credentials and my 30 years of experience with three major corporations.

These are only a few of the reasons I am qualified for the position. The enclosed resume lists additional responsibilities and accomplishments from my career. I look forward to the opportunity to discuss how I can help your company achieve its growth and profit goals.

Sincerely,

Leo Bonnell

1324 Chestnut Court
Boston, MA 09877
Leo.Bonnell@xxx.com

Bob McDougall
34 Eirie Street
Davenport, IA 56778

May 6, 20___

Lester Jones
Carson Construction
23 Elm Street
Davenport, IA 55693

Dear Mr. Jones:

I was very impressed by the article about Carson Construction in the November 8th *Davenport Times*. Your record of sales growth over the past five years is enviable, and I think your diversification moves have been strategically sound.

I believe that my experience in similar environments would be valuable to a company such as Carson. I know how to design and implement management control systems that enable companies to sustain growth in profits along with growth in sales. This can be done without putting unnecessary restraints on the ability to exploit emerging opportunities.

The enclosed resume gives specifics on several of my accomplishments in this field. I would like to meet with you to see whether my skills and experience might match a need you have within your organization. I will follow up next week to request an appointment.

Sincerely,

Bob McDougall

✛ **John Fitzgerald**
2 Gotham Street
Detroit, MI 54663

July 7, 20__

David Schuster
Gotham Industries
445 Milk Street
Detroit, MI 55677

Dear Mr. Schuster,

I am writing you concerning your openings in customer service and sales. As my resume outlines, I have had extensive experience in these functions.

Some of my accomplishments include the following:

• Directed development of a Fortune 500 company's five-year strategic plan.
• Developed and presented marketing proposals to the corporate executive committee.
• Conducted a market research study on the commercialization of catalysts manufactured in space for a major aerospace firm.
• Created and managed the customer service department for a major manufacturer.
• Designed operational flowcharts, tracking systems, and productivity measurements.

My background has been very successful in diverse and challenging environments. I look forward to meeting you in person to discuss how my talents can lead to superior results for you. I will call you next week to arrange a convenient time.

Sincerely,

John Fitzgerald

Margaret Carson
5 Willow Road • Gulf Shores, AL 44564

September 5, 20__

Karen Barnes
KBS Financial Services
123 Altoona Drive
Gulf Shores, AL 44567

Dear Ms. Barnes:

A mutual friend, Sharon Greisse, suggested I contact you concerning potential accounting openings within your organization.

After raising a family of four, I returned to college and completed my undergraduate degree in accounting in 2002. Since then I have been an accounting supervisor with Trasco Industries in Huntsville. Unfortunately the cutback in the automotive parts industry has affected our profitability, and the company will be consolidating its operations in Dallas in June. Since I wish to remain in Alabama, I declined the company's offer to relocate to Texas.

I would welcome the opportunity to meet with you in the near future to discuss any opportunities that may exist within your organization or to discuss other leads of which you may be aware.

I'll call your office next week to follow up. Thank you in advance for your time and consideration.

Sincerely,

Margaret Carson

Jamil King
955 East Elm Street, #631
New York, NY 10006
April 4, 20__

Mark Edwards
Cordell Bank
7 Schooner Way
St. Louis, MO 65445

Dear Mr. Edwards:

I recently read in the Washington University alumni letter that you were in need of a senior lending officer. Over the past 20 years I have worked as a relationship officer for three of New York's premier commercial banks.

My family and I have decided to relocate to the St. Louis area to live closer to my wife's elderly parents. I am very interested in opportunities at Cordell Bank due to its excellent reputation in the industry.

I've enclosed a copy of my resume, which further outlines my background and experience. I'll call next week to determine if it will be possible to meet during the week of May 5th, during my upcoming trip to St. Louis.

Best wishes,

Jamil King

Jose Hernandez

5 Federal Ave

Boston, MA 09887

(617) 555-9817 • J.Hernandez@xxx.com

May 6, 20__

Tom Jones
Bradley's Inc.
222 Spring St.
Boston, MA 07887

Dear Mr. Jones:

I am forwarding you the enclosed resume in response to your ad in the *Boston Globe*. The ad was of particular interest to me since the described requirements closely match my experience and expertise.

I have had extensive experience in material handling and the purchasing of commodity products. I have negotiated contracts of this nature since 1990 and have a proven track record of reducing costs.

Based on my experience and the requirements described in the ad, I feel that I can be a valuable asset to your company. I look forward to talking further with you in the near future.

Sincerely,

Jose Hernandez

MILDRED PEARSE

4 Tall Timber Drive
Bethesda, MD 20112

June 4, 20__

Tom James
Thompson Products
123 West Street
Bethesda, MD 20011

Dear Mr. James:

I have had the pleasure of using many of your fine products over the past twenty years. Your reputation for excellence in products and people makes your company the type of organization I would like to join.

For the past twenty-six years I have held positions in sales and customer service. My skills include fifteen years' experience working with the most up-to-date database programs, high-speed printers, and inventory control systems. I also have successfully recruited new customers, handled customer service issues, and improved our company's relations with the local community.

I would appreciate the opportunity to meet with you to discuss how my qualifications can meet your needs. I will email you next week to arrange a meeting. Thank you for your time and consideration.

Sincerely,

Mildred Pearse

Tom Luskin
123 Day Street
Buffalo, NY 33456

July 6, 20__

Janice Jackson
BAPCO Incorporated
23 Way Drive
Buffalo, NY 33456

Dear Ms. Jackson:

Peter Hampton suggested I contact you about marketing opportunities within your organization. I am particularly interested in your company because of its fine reputation and commitment to growth and excellence.

I am a seasoned manager with strong credentials. My experience includes the areas of planning, operations, and customer service. I have a history of substantial accomplishments in banking and manufacturing reflecting my sound decision-making and analytical skills.

Throughout my employment history I have exhibited excellent interpersonal skills, been a solid team player, and utilized both verbal and written communication skills with all levels of employees and management.

I am flexible on relocation and start dates. I look forward to discussing my assets and skills with you in detail.

Sincerely,

Tom Luskin

Amir Singh

5 Nanio Drive
Spartanburg, SC 56554

April 8, 20__

Lester Long
Arcadia Mills
377 Ridgeway Drive
Spartanburg, SC 55689

Dear Mr. Long:

A friend, Beth Gill, recently informed me about the opening in your marketing department and suggested that I email you directly. I would like to be considered for the position of Marketing Manager.

As the attached resume indicates, since graduating from the University of South Carolina, I have spent my career marketing consumer goods products. In each company I have been responsible for purchasing marketing research and developing strategic marketing initiatives. Most recently, I have commissioned studies of both the U.S. retail markets and the bulk commodity goods industry.

Based on my background in marketing and marketing research, I believe I have the capabilities you are looking for. I would like to explore this opportunity more completely in a personal interview. I look forward to hearing from you at your convenience.

Sincerely,

Amir Singh

(864) 555-2272
A.Singh@xxx.com

Yuki Shimura

6 Young Street
Los Angeles, CA 98773

July 7, 20__

David Alan
Jones Consulting
556 Glengo Drive
Los Angeles, CA 98767

Dear Mr. Alan:

Jack Jones suggested I contact you concerning assistance with a career change. I am a highly experienced industrial engineer looking for a position with a firm that understands what it takes to succeed in today's marketplace.

As the enclosed resume illustrates, I offer a solid background in both manufacturing and engineering, with more than 30 years of experience in a variety of working environments.

In a recent situation, a decision was made to set up a manufacturing cell to eliminate serious efficiency problems in a plastic extruding process. I organized the group and then developed and implemented the program. Production increased by 45 percent, and the floor space required for the process was reduced by 22 percent.

I would greatly appreciate any information or referrals you could provide. I am convinced that networking will be the key to successfully finding the right position. Can we get together for twenty minutes sometime next week? I will call you in the next several days to schedule an appointment at your convenience.

Sincerely,

Yuki Shimura

LINDA POWELL
4 Rutland Street
Chicago, IL 60603

June 4, 20__

Bob Lenny
Hansen Foods
34 Board Street
Chicago, IL 60601

Dear Mr. Lenny:

Your classified advertisement in the *Tribune* was of interest to me. The knowledge and experience I gained through 20 years of experience at Eastern Telecom closely matches your requirements.

As my resume shows, I have had progressively more responsibility in the field of human resources. I concentrate in, but am not limited to, the areas of compensation, manpower planning, and benefits.

During my experience I have exhibited excellent interpersonal skills, developed strong computer knowledge, been a solid team player, and utilized both verbal and written communications skills to all levels of employees and management.

I look forward to having the opportunity to talk further with you in the near future.

Best wishes,

Linda Powell

Tim Hester

7 Park Avenue
New York, NY 10121
(212) 555-0910
Tim.Hester@xxx.com

March 6, 20__

Jack Jones
Jones Recruiting
123 Algen Way
New York, NY 10122

Dear Mr. Jones:

I am seeking a senior-level management position in marketing with a consumer products company. I have had more than twenty-five years of successful management experience in one of the most competitive industries in the world.

In my most recent job as National Director of Marketing for Drake Beverage, I took a $40 million brand from a $1.5 million loss to a $1 million profit in eighteen months. Sales exceeded forecast by 12 percent in the most recent quarter.

I have a preference for the Northeast, but I will consider relocation to other areas of the country. While the challenge of the job and opportunities for advancement are my primary concerns, you should be aware that my compensation has been in the $100,000–$105,000 range.

Please let me know if you are working on any searches requiring someone with my qualifications. It would be a pleasure to discuss my background with you in person, by email, or over the phone. Thank you for your time and consideration.

Sincerely,

Tim Hester

ANDY FREIDENBERG
56 Young Street
Omaha, NE 55698

May 7, 20__

Commissioner Arnold Stranley
Lincoln County
234 Main Street
Omaha, NE 55699

Dear Commissioner Stranley:

I have been a resident of Lincoln County for more than 20 years, and for most of those years I have been employed within the county. I am writing to ask for your help. As a knowledgeable leader in the county's efforts to bring additional industry to Lincoln, you may be aware of organizations in need of proven talent in manufacturing.

Recently I turned down an opportunity for advancement in my company because it meant moving to Florida. For a variety of reasons I wish to stay in Lincoln County, Nebraska, where my family is rooted.

The enclosed resume illustrates my progression of increasingly responsible assignments since graduating from college in 1981. I am most interested in a position as an Assistant Plant Manager for a medium-size manufacturing operation.

I would like to meet with you to discuss companies or people I might be able to talk with in my search. I will follow up next week to request an appointment.

Sincerely,

Andy Freidenberg

Jerry Fandango

5 Bull Street

Houston, TX 24332

April 1, 20___

Mark Carl
Jennings Corporation
123 Willow Springs
Houston, TX 23998

Dear Mr. Carl:

Jennings Corporation has an excellent reputation in the mining industry and is known for their quality products. Due to a recent downsizing at Gorman Products, I am currently seeking a position in quality control in an organization like yours. I believe I can make a valuable contribution to your company by using my years of experience to help further your rapid growth and good service.

As a quality control inspector I have worked with many different types of products. I am particularly experienced with CNC programming and LATH 260s and 298s, which I know are your specialties.

I will call you early next week to set up an appointment to discuss employment opportunities. I look forward to speaking with you in further detail with you then.

Sincerely,

Jerry Fandango

Leslie Stewart
27 Palm Blvd. • Miami, FL 20997

March 5, 20__

John Riley
Tasco Systems
45 Broad Street
Miami, FL 20996

Dear Mr. Riley:

Your name was given to me by Ben Smith at Olsen Manufacturing. He spoke highly of you and felt that your broad expertise and knowledge could be helpful to me.

My company has been experiencing a series of reorganizations and layoffs. Rather than accepting a transfer that might not utilize my abilities to their fullest, I decided that this would be an excellent time to find a position that represents a first-class opportunity to contribute.

My background includes management of several different operational areas, including financial and administrative. I am knowledgeable in accounting systems and staff management and would be interested to learn your perceptions of how my background might fit into your industry.

I plan to call you next week to arrange a mutually convenient time to meet.

Sincerely,

Leslie Stewart

(305) 555-0889
L.Stewart@xxx.com

BECKY FLYNN

5 Young Avenue

Wichita, KS 74667

(316) 555-0388

September 5, 20__

Jason Roberts

Pierce Department Stores

45 Lucky Street

Wichita, KS 77658

Dear Mr. Roberts:

After more than 30 years of successful experience in retail, I am seeking a new position in which my abilities can be utilized more fully.

As you can see from the attached resume, my record is one of increasing responsibility. My most recent employer has favorably commented on my in-depth knowledge of its retail plans and the assistance the company has received from my efforts.

If you see a possible fit with your organization, I would like to meet with you for an exploratory discussion. I'll plan to call you next week to see when we might get together.

Sincerely,

Becky Flynn